# PRISON LIFE AMONG THE REBELS

Henry S. White, chaplain, from *History of the Fifth Regiment of Rhode Island Heavy Artillery, January 1862–June 1865* (Providence, 1892).

# Prison Life
# among the Rebels

## Recollections of a Union Chaplain

*Edited by*
*Edward D. Jervey*

THE KENT STATE UNIVERSITY PRESS
Kent, Ohio, and London, England

©1990 by The Kent State University Press, Kent, Ohio 44242
All rights reserved
Library of Congress Catalog Card Number 89-39689
ISBN 0-87338-403-2
ISBN 0-87338-404-0
Manufactured in the United States of America

Portions of this work appeared earlier in somewhat different form and are reproduced here with permission:
"Ten Weeks in a Macon Prison, 1864: A New England Chaplain's Account," *Georgia Historical Quarterly* 70 (Winter 1986): 669–702; "Prison Life among the Rebels: Recollections of a Union Chaplain," *Civil War History* (March 1988): 22–45.

**Library of Congress Cataloging-in-Publication Data**
White, Henry S., 1828–1916.
    Prison life among the rebels : recollections of a Union chaplain / edited by Edward D. Jervey.
       p.   cm.
    Includes bibliographical references.
    ISBN 0-87338-403-2. ∞ —ISBN 87338-404-0 (pbk.) ∞
    1. White, Henry S., 1828–1916—Correspondence. 2. United States—History—Civil War, 1861–1865—Prisoners and prisons. 3. United States—History—Civil War, 1861–1865—Personal narratives. 4. United States—History—Civil War, 1861–1865—Chaplains. 5. Chaplains, Military—United States—Correspondence. I. Jervey, Edward Drewry, 1929– . II. Title.
E611.W5 1990
973.7'71—dc20                                89-39689
                                             CIP

British Library Cataloging-in-Publication data are available.

For James Harvey Young—
inspiring teacher, magnificent scholar,
and true friend

# Contents

Preface . . . . . . . . . . . . . . . . . . . . . . . . . . . . . . . . . . . . . . . . . . . . . . . . . . . . . . . ix

Introduction . . . . . . . . . . . . . . . . . . . . . . . . . . . . . . . . . . . . . . . . . . . . . . . . . xi

Letter 1 . . . . . . . . . . . . . . . . . . . . . . . . . . . . . . . . . . . . . . . . . . . . . . . . . . . . . 1

Letter 2 . . . . . . . . . . . . . . . . . . . . . . . . . . . . . . . . . . . . . . . . . . . . . . . . . . . . . 6

Letter 3 . . . . . . . . . . . . . . . . . . . . . . . . . . . . . . . . . . . . . . . . . . . . . . . . . . . . . 11

Letter 4 . . . . . . . . . . . . . . . . . . . . . . . . . . . . . . . . . . . . . . . . . . . . . . . . . . . . . 16

Letter 5 . . . . . . . . . . . . . . . . . . . . . . . . . . . . . . . . . . . . . . . . . . . . . . . . . . . . . 22

Letter 6 . . . . . . . . . . . . . . . . . . . . . . . . . . . . . . . . . . . . . . . . . . . . . . . . . . . . . 28

Letter 7 . . . . . . . . . . . . . . . . . . . . . . . . . . . . . . . . . . . . . . . . . . . . . . . . . . . . . 33

Letter 8 . . . . . . . . . . . . . . . . . . . . . . . . . . . . . . . . . . . . . . . . . . . . . . . . . . . . . 37

Letter 9 . . . . . . . . . . . . . . . . . . . . . . . . . . . . . . . . . . . . . . . . . . . . . . . . . . . . . 41

Letter 10 . . . . . . . . . . . . . . . . . . . . . . . . . . . . . . . . . . . . . . . . . . . . . . . . . . . . 45

Letter 11 . . . . . . . . . . . . . . . . . . . . . . . . . . . . . . . . . . . . . . . . . . . . . . . . . . . . 49

Letter 12 . . . . . . . . . . . . . . . . . . . . . . . . . . . . . . . . . . . . . . . . . . . . . . . . . . . . 54

Letter 13 . . . . . . . . . . . . . . . . . . . . . . . . . . . . . . . . . . . . . . . . . . . . . . . . . . . . 58

Letter 14 . . . . . . . . . . . . . . . . . . . . . . . . . . . . . . . . . . . . . . . . . . . . . . . . . . . . 62

Letter 15 . . . . . . . . . . . . . . . . . . . . . . . . . . . . . . . . . . . . . . . . . . . . . . . . . . . . 66

Letter 16 . . . . . . . . . . . . . . . . . . . . . . . . . . . . . . . . . . . . . . . . . . . . . . . . . . . . 71

Letter 17 . . . . . . . . . . . . . . . . . . . . . . . . . . . . . . . . . . . . . . . . . . . . . . . . . . . . 76

Letter 18 . . . . . . . . . . . . . . . . . . . . . . . . . . . . . . . . . . . . . . . . . . . . . . . . . . . . 81

Epilogue . . . . . . . . . . . . . . . . . . . . . . . . . . . . . . . . . . . . . . . . . . . . . . . . . . . . 85

Notes . . . . . . . . . . . . . . . . . . . . . . . . . . . . . . . . . . . . . . . . . . . . . . . . . . . . . . . 86

Index . . . . . . . . . . . . . . . . . . . . . . . . . . . . . . . . . . . . . . . . . . . . . . . . . . . . . . . 93

# *Preface*

The remarkable letters of Henry S. White were happily discovered while researching the history of *Zion's Herald,* a fiercely independent Methodist newspaper founded in 1823 and widely read throughout New York and New England. White, an ordained Methodist minister, was appointed a Northern chaplain in 1863. Captured the next year, he spent over three months as a prisoner. During the next eight months after his release, he wrote eighteen letters to the *Herald* detailing his experiences.

A number of people helped to make this book possible. Ann Greene Whiting, editor of *Zion's Herald,* gave me inestimable help in checking certain aspects of the letters. Robin Hoffman of Radford University library gave much of her time in obtaining needed books and microfilm. Carolyn Sutphin, also of Radford University, spent a tremendous number of hours in typing the manuscript through its several stages. John Inscoe of the *Georgia Historical Quarterly* initially encouraged the publication of the letters dealing with Macon prison. John Hubbell, editor of *Civil War History* and director of the Kent State University Press, encouraged the publication of all of White's letters and supervised the project throughout. Laurel Brandt of the Kent State University Press was a great help also in the final stage of preparation.

Dr. James I. Robertson, Jr., read the first draft and made critically necessary suggestions as well as supplying a large number of notes for names and facts. Several people furnished a detailed chronology of White's ministry: Charles A. Bass, Jr., research assistant, Boston University School of Theology; the Reverend Richard O'Neill, Wisconsin Conference Commission on

Archives and History; and the Reverend Ronald A. Brunger, Archivist, Detroit Annual Conference. Finally, my wife, Thora Jo, was my best critic and proofreader, not only with this work but throughout thirty years of academia. Without her encouragement, this and other projects would never have been accomplished.

# *Introduction*

Chaplains in the Civil War, both North and South, were a mixed lot. Some were disliked intensely because they neglected their spiritual duties, some were fearful of battles, and some did not truly share the hard lot of camps with the soldiers. Yet others were held in high esteem because they attended to their primary duties and, as the war progressed, went with their men into the dangerous zones of battle to minister to their spiritual needs. Many other good men would have remained, but the pay was often so meager that they could not afford to stay in service and still try to care for their families. The chaplains always posed a problem for the rival governments, for the idea of keeping ministers incarcerated did not set well with either side. Orders and counterorders were issued throughout most of the period 1862–64 in regard to releasing such prisoners.[1]

Very few records of chaplains have been published. One is that of the Reverend Frederic Denison, who wrote of his experiences in the Union Army.[2] Denison and others like him, some of whom were captured and imprisoned, were in all likelihood held in high respect by most of the men, for these chaplains had indeed attended to their primary duties and, risking capture, accompanied the men into the battle zones.

Another such chaplain, a friend of Denison, has left us a remarkable record of life during captivity. Henry S. White was born in 1828 at North Hoosick, New York. He was the son of Newman Sumner White and Abigail Stark, a granddaughter of Captain John Stark, who commanded a company of militia at the battle of Bennington. White became an apprentice blacksmith to his father, then decided to go to Concord, New Hampshire to attend the Methodist Biblical Institute. He graduated in 1851, and for the next eleven years served various churches in the Providence Conference of the Methodist Episcopal Church. In January 1863, while pastor of the Broadway Methodist Episcopal Church in Providence, he was appointed chaplain of the Rhode Island Regiment Heavy Artillery, then serving in North Carolina.[3]

White quickly endeared himself to his regiment by virtue of his spirit and devotion to his duties. New Berne, North Carolina, had been taken by Union forces in March 1862, and things remained relatively quiet until mid-March 1863. Dissatisfied with inactivity in North Carolina, Confederate authorities in Richmond had ordered a portion of Longstreet's corps of the Army of North Virginia into North Carolina. Over the next six weeks, skirmishes occurred between both forces, but New Berne remained in Union control. During this time White continued ministering to the men with much diligence.

In the summer of 1863, White went home on furlough, returning with a stand of colors from the Forty-fourth Massachusetts to present to his Rhode Island regiment. He told his regiment "The name of the gallant Fifth and its noble officers and men, I am proud to tell you, has gone not only to Rhode Island, but throughout New England, and I may say throughout the whole North. Everywhere I received the most courteous attention, because of my connection with you and your service."[4]

During the fall and early winter matters remained calm around New Berne. In March 1864 the Confederates took up the attack again, but with the opening of the Virginia campaign as many Confederates as could be spared hurried north. However, a large cavalry force remained. On May 4, 1864, White received permission to visit Croatan Station, a small fort on the railroad east of New Berne, to distribute tracts and letters to Federal troops there. The next day, in a surprise attack by the Confederate forces, he was captured.

White's eighteen letters to *Zion's Herald* detail the period from his capture in May 1864 through his release in September 1864. The first seven letters contain his observations on the South as well as his capture at Croatan, subsequent forced march to Kinston, North Carolina, and his removal to Georgia. In letters eight, nine, and ten, White recounts his one-day stay at Andersonville.

Letters eleven through fifteen and part of sixteen detail White's experiences at Macon. The officer's prison at Macon, ninety miles northeast of

Andersonville, is not as well known as Andersonville, although many former prisoners published accounts of their experiences there.[5] The prison was built early in 1864 to quarter all captured Union officers, many of whom were to be transferred there from both Andersonville and Libby Prison in Richmond. Reports from Andersonville, though, indicate that many officers who wished to remain with their troops managed to stay there either through deception or Confederate negligence. John McElroy, an Andersonville survivor, reported that between two hundred and three hundred captains and lieutenants spent several weeks there passing themselves off as enlisted men they had commanded before they were eventually sent to Macon.[6]

Macon was always considered vulnerable to attack. Both General John Winder, Andersonville's commandant, and General Howell Cobb, commander of the Georgia Reserves headquartered in Macon, reported that the prison was not secure and Confederate forces were too small to protect it. A prison riot in June was prevented only because the camp commander had been secretly warned of it.[7] Perhaps because the Macon prison was in operation for such a short time and held relatively few prisoners, its sanitary facilities were always inadequate, although never as horrible as at Andersonville. A stream flowed through the Macon camp, but water was always scarce, and "vermin" plagued prisoners everywhere—in their clothes and their quarters. When White arrived at Macon in mid-May, the prison was still incomplete.

The remainder of White's letters detail his removal to Savannah and thence to Charleston and his final release.

Because no other diary, journal, or letters regarding White's captivity have been found, it is uncertain whether his letters to *Zion's Herald* were written strictly from memory or from notes he made and was able to hide while a prisoner. If the latter is true, he made no reference to such notes. The datelines of the letters, as published in *Zion's Herald,* indicate that they were composed and submitted during and just after his final weeks of service with his regiment as the war drew to an end. The dates at the beginning of each letter indicate when White wrote them; the dates at the end indicate the date of publication in *Zion's Herald.*[8]

Some grammatical changes have been made for the sake of readability, but White's misspellings have been left intact. Periodically White's very strong anti-Southern biases warped his judgment, as well as his memory. His opinions should not be confused with facts.

# PRISON LIFE AMONG THE REBELS

# &ô Letter 1

Providence, R.I., Oct. 20, 1864

My Dear *Herald:* —You cannot imagine how I missed your good old intelligent, familiar face during the long weary months of my captivity. For almost five long months I saw no *Zion's Herald.* For sixteen months I had not been North to take by the hand those good men who mould and shape you for the public feast. Something about these days in Dixie I propose to tell you. By making you my confidant I shall also speak some words of greeting to old friends who may be asking if (as they say in the army) "he has gone up." No, no my good friend, I have not gone up yet, although, thank God, someday I hope to. I still live a good thrifty life in the flesh, and, what is better, that other life lives and thrives in me day by day and more and more. In this paper I will note some loose facts, open the way for my correspondence, and in my next commence my narrative and follow it to its close.

I was captured, May 5, at Croatan, eleven miles from Newbern, N.C.,[1] and taken to Kinston, Goldsboro, Wilmington, Branchville, Macon, Andersonville, Savannah and Charleston. I have seen much, covered much, with officers, privates, citizens and Negroes, and have enjoyed the privilege of inspecting the great revolt from the inside.

On September 23, I was taken from under fire at Charleston, where we had been for twenty-one days, and on the rebel steamer *Celt* taken down the harbor past the ruins at Fort Sumter, and other works of lesser note, to the truce ground. Here we met the United States steamer, *Delaware,* and were soon transferred on board, and came under the protection of the government and beneath a flag proud and noble and worth perserving. Some of the impressions I received, I deem important in the present state of the country.

First, I think the rebellion near its end. I draw this conclusion from several facts: The men of the South that intend to go in the army are now in it, and those who are not in it have left the country. The soldiers expect the strife to close soon, and if it does not they say they will leave. Davis says two thirds of his army are absent without leave.[2] What is to prevent the other third from following?

Second, the chief and last hope of the rebels is in the "Peace men" of the North. They did look to Cotton, to England and France, to God, to their own right arms, but in their papers and in conversations with me they seem mostly to have abandoned all those grounds of confidence and now look to the defeat of Lincoln and the election of McClellan. The rebels are solid for McClellan. They sought to pledge me to vote for him.

Third, the rebels will not arm the Negroes.[3] I may be mistaken in this; I think I am not. I conversed with many of their officers and men of rank. Some freely told me they could not trust the Negroes with arms. I met one gentleman who had several hundred slaves, and was a member of the legislature of his State, who told me that the South would arm its slaves, but said that the whole system of the army would have to be changed to do it. He said that each master would have to organize, drill and fight his own slaves. He thought the slaves would be true to their owners, but did not think another man could manage them. This same man, although one of the strongest secessionists, was entirely despondent about their final success.

Fourth, the Negroes are loyal to the North. I never met one that did not understand this struggle.[4] I never met one that I spoke to on the subject that was not loyal to the Yankees, as they all call us. I have often employed them, and not one ever deceived me. On more than one occasion, I have had reason to be grateful for favors. I shall give many facts in future papers. I cannot refer to them now.

Fifth, such Union men as I met, and there were many, all go for the election of Lincoln.[5] They say that if he is elected the rebels will give up. They urge us to hold on and be firm, and the thing will soon be over.

Sixth, the foreigners of the South are heart and soul with us. They talk it, they act it. It would do your heart good to hear some of the Irish women talk about that "divil of a Jiff Davis," and "good Mr. Lincoln."

Seventh, the States have no common bond of sympathy between them. They will not take Georgia money in South Carolina. The soldiers mock and jeer at each other, and there seems to be no bond of sympathy and union between them. The doctrine of States Rights has produced its legitimate fruits. The people of the South have little reverence for any general government, ours or Jeff's. They go for the sovereignty of the States.[6] Do you ask wherein lies the strength of the Confederate Government? I answer, Davis has got control of the States' armies. The strength of the rebellion is its army. Press that so as to break it up and allow the troops from each State to go home, and the rebellion is gone. One morning after the fall of Atlanta I said to one of the rebels, "Well, sir, do you know that Sherman and Brown are going to take Georgia back into the Union?" "I hope to God they will," said he. "What will you do?" "Do? I'll go home." "But you can't go home." "I'll *go*," said he. "Do your men ever get away?" "Yes," said he; "the other night eighteen went, and they caught three and sent three officers after the others, but neither officers nor privates ever turned up." "Where did they go?" "Go? They went to Sherman." "Do you go with your State?" "To be sure I do." "Suppose Georgia goes back into the old Union, what will you do?" "I will go with her." "But suppose the Confederate Government makes war on Georgia for going back, what will you do?" "Then I'll fight for the United States." These thoughts I wish at once to fling out for what good they may be.

Large quantities of boxes and bundles for the officers and privates were put on board the *Celt,* and then we gladly moved away. Past the monitors and ships of every mould and strength we swept, toward Hilton Head. Soon we were invited to the tables spread as God's people into God's land know how to do. It has been my custom to say grace on sitting down to eat. As I leaned my head upon my hand and silently lifted my heart in gratitude, I trust the Lord saw in me a contrite and humble heart. Sixteen hundred officers of our army, and from thirty to forty thousand privates, good men and true, were left in the hands of the most godless and merciless set of tyrants, and to a fate of suffering beyond the conception of those who do not see it. Daily and hourly, do I remember them, and wish I could share with them my bread and meat. Some of the party were full of mirth and fun. One took up the knife and silver fork beside his plate, and turning to the associate said, "Doctor, what are these?" "Well," said his comrade, "I don't know what they are." Then he cooly laid them one side and begun to use his hands for the food. All was mirth and good cheer. It was not a little queer to have dishes and a table-cloth and mirrors, and chairs to sit in.

Night came on before we reached Hilton Head, and we remained on the steamer that night, and in the morning we proceeded to the Port Royal House. Here we were at once inspected. Inspections, you are doubtless aware, form an important item in military affairs. The inspecting officer into whose hands I fell, chanced to be my good friend and fellow laborer, Chaplain Denison,[7] of the Third Rhode Island Heavy Artillery. After the usual salute and a good hearty shake of the hand, he proceeded like a good soldier to his work. "Look here," said he, "what is all this fringe about your coat? Then there is the button gone. What, no vest and no shirt?" My calvary boots had contributed their tops to a reb, who one day insisted on having them for the sum of five dollars Confederate money. The toes and old soles were left me. "What, no stockings?" said he, as he examined the marching department. The pants bore evidence of cunning needlework. In front the ventilation was ample, as became a hot country. The rear had at sundry times and in increasing quantities gone on detached service. My hat had "gone up." A cap in the tip of the style, topped out the Chaplain. Rev. Charles Dixon, a local preacher and chaplain of the 16th Connecticut Regiment, was my worthy and noble co-laborer and co-sufferer.[8] Whether he in garb looked more like a Christian than your humble servant, I cannot tell. The inspection, however, resulted in an order to fall in at once and proceed with Br. Denison to his headquarters and the Christian Commission Rooms, where we were soon put in a more presentable trim. Right heartily did he laugh at us for attempting to represent the cloth with no cloth on our back. Almost five months had passed in the custody of the enemies of God and all good. Sixteen months before, after my usual furlough, I had left a fond good wife and four children, beloved and dear to me, to go again to the army and help save the good flag, and I had not looked upon them in all those weary months. Just before my captivity I heard they were well. During those five months I heard not a word. I took passage on a steamer for Providence, and seeing a friend from near my home, my heart beat quick as I said, "Is my family well?" "They are all well," said he. My voice grew husky and tears stood in my eyes, and my heart sent grateful thanksgiving up to God. "Does your wife know you are coming?" "She does not know I have escaped from prison," I said. "You should have sent a telegram." Then I told him my reason. Several times I sought to obtain a leave of absence, and when I expected to come home I sent word. I could not go. Charley said, "Mamma, tell father he does not tell true. He said he was coming home, and he did not come." Then I said, "I will go when I can, but will send no word." In the morning he offered to call and give my wife a hint of my coming. Entering my house so early and in great good nature, and not seeming to have any errand, [my] wife soon began to mistrust. "Have you heard from my husband?" "Yes." "Has he been released from the hands of the rebels?" "Yes, he has got out." "Where is he?" "He was in New York, yesterday." "Yesterday? Where is he now?" "He is on his way home." "On his way home? Is he in this city?" "Yes, he is down at the armory, and will soon be up." Reader, have you been to the war, and after toil and suffering returned to the embrace of a family that God had kept? Then you can finish the picture of sunshine amid the shadows of war. Have you stayed at home when the shell hissed and the flag was torn, and there was no bread and no meat? Words could not show you the antechamber of heaven that was in my home.

*Zion's Herald and Wesleyan Journal,* November 2, 1864, p. 173. (The newspaper used this full title in 1864 and 1865.)

# ✄ *Letter 2*

Providence, R.I., Oct. 28, 1864

A chaplain's work is peculiar, and much of it, if he would do the most good possible, must be of a pastoral character. Preaching as a general thing must be a brief and occasional work. Often a regiment is in such circumstances that a chance is afforded for preaching to the regiment in a body, but in some areas of the service, the whole regiment is never together. My regiment being heavy artillery is separated, the companies being in several forts separated from each other, from one to many miles. The method I have adopted for serving the men is to preach to detachments when opportunity serves. To visit the regimental hospital daily, or when the state of the men seemed to demand my presence. To hold social services two or three times in the week in the hospital, others besides the sick coming in if they choose to do so. We were accustomed to have a religious service each afternoon at dress parade; but my chief work was to go weekly from tent to tent with the papers and tracts furnished by the Christian Commission, and distribute them to the men.[1] I could often say words for Jesus, and my soul was filled with exceeding comfort. The men received me most cordially, and I have found a tent or a picket post to be a sanctuary of God.

It was on one of these pastoral tours that I was captured. The circumstances run thus: On the afternoon of the 4th of May I filled the saddle bags of my saddle with books and tracts, and strapped a good bundle on my horse besides, and started for Croatan, a station on the Railroad from Newbern to Beaufort, eleven miles away. I rode along the road in quiet that was so soon to be filled with the enemy. All was still, and not the murmur of danger was heard. I passed our pickets, finding them in good cheer, and reached the fort about 4 o'clock, P.M. Captain Aigan,[2] of the 5th Rhode Island, with Lieut. Durfee[3] and the members of Company A, I found well. I went to each tent giving papers and wrote of good cheer and holy counsel; I knew not then it was my last visit for many months, and to many of them, my last visit on earth. The evening hours I spent in a ride out to the bank of the Neuse River, to a plantation occupied by an old friend from Providence. Lieutenant Durfee was my companion, and it was well dark before we reached the picket. Giving the countersign, we passed on to the fort. I remained that night with Capt. Aigan, Lieut. Durfee kindly compelling me to sleep in his bed while he composed himself in a blanket on the floor.

Capt. Aigan was up when I awoke, which was occasioned by the exciting voice and tales of a negro woman near the tent. She said the rebs were near her house cutting out a barricade of trees that our forces had felled across a road leading back into the rebel country. This barricade was intended to keep back cavalry and artillery, and to impede and hinder the advance of infantry. The negroes lived about this region, and had been permitted to make turpentine in the pine forests. Not much credence was given to her story, as no force was just then expected, or if in the mist of the morning she did see persons at work at the blockade, we supposed it might be the negroes who were trying to open the way to get their turpentine out. Capt. Aigan did not eat many moments when he arose from the table and went out to look around. At this time another negro came, confirming the statement of the former. She said a sentinel with a musket was posted near her house, and that many men were at work on the trees with axes. This crossing of "Brice's Creek" was through a swamp and rough road, and so bad a place to cross a body of troops that but little fear of an advance from this direction was apprehended. When we were told of the advance we did not believe they would come on this road; but to know the true state of the case, Sergeant Kenneday [*sic*] with a dozen men was sent on a reconnaisance to the place.[4] On another road leading in the same direction into the back country, we had a picket nearly two miles from the fort. Capt. Aigan mounted his horse and went out to visit this picket and see if it had been disturbed. He had proceeded but a short distance through the woods before he found himself just upon a number of the enemy, and wheeling his horse made the best use of his spurs and his wits in beating

7

a retreat. The rebels shouted, "head off that man, head off that man," but as they wished to capture him they did not fire. The Captain made good time on his way to the fort. Sergeant Kenneday and his party soon came from their scout and reported the enemy coming in force. No one was hurt in the skirmish, but some of the men on picket were driven into the woods, and did not come in till the action was over.

On his arrival at the fort Capt. Aigan gave orders for the tents to be struck, water and food to be taken inside the work, and all preparation made for defense. My horse had been saddled early in the morning as I intended to go to Newbern in the cool of the day, but choosing not to go till I saw how things were going, my horse and the one connected with the work were sent round to a rifle pit in the rear where they would be more safe than in any other position. The drawbridge was removed, gate shut, and all took shelter in the fort. The fort was a small irregular earthwork, with only one six pound brass gun beside the muskets of the men for its defense. The garrison numbered about fifty men. About forty-five were in the work. The preparations had not long been completed when the enemy made his appearance on the Railroad nearly a mile distant, between us and Newbern. They came down toward us rapidly and without fear, and in considerable force. As soon as they were in clear view, Capt. Aigan ordered a shell to be thrown, which struck close to a horse in the advance. Another and another were got into their midst before they could halt the column and recover from the confusion, for they were evidently not expecting shells just then. They deployed rapidly to the left and disappeared among the trees. We continued to fire on them till they were out of sight. So accurate was our fire, that as we fired on the colors one shell passed between the staff and the man's head who bore it.

Sending out a man to reconnoitre, he soon returned and informed us they were dismounting. Presently we saw skirmishers cross the Railroad to the right, and not long after a brisk fire was opened upon us from an old house and the adjacent woods. We at once returned the fire with the piece and the muskets. Gradually the line of fire was extended till we were entirely surrounded. For six and a half hours the firing was rapid and continuous. The enemy came within a few rods under cover of an old rifle pit. Before long my horse was struck and fell.[5] Solid shot, shell and canister were thrown first in one direction and then in another, and as our cannon was a field piece and mounted on an elevated platform, it commanded the approach in every direction. In using it the men were ordered to keep well down to escape the rebel fire. The muskets also did their part of the work; the sharpshooters from the trees were more annoying than from any other position; the piece became so hot that it was almost impossible to work it; the water began to give out, and the cartridges began to take fire when put in the mouth of the piece, throwing the gunners against the wall of the fort. For more than an hour before the action ceased, the men were compelled to handle their muskets by the gunslings.

As I went around among the men to cheer, help, or do anything I could (and thank good fortune I did find a spot where I could do a little), I was more than ever impressed with the patriotism of the noble men who compose our army. Capt. Aigan was cool and brave, and nobly did he perform his duty. Lieut. Durfee superintended the ammunition, and was constantly at his post. At half past two o'clock a white flag was seen coming down the Railroad; firing ceased on both sides. Capt. Aigan went out to meet it and asked what was wanted, if it was a mere show to enable him to get a better position. The reply [was] that the surrender of the fort was demanded. Capt. Aigan replied that he could not surrender the fort. He was then informed that it would be reduced, as complete preparations were at hand for the purpose; but if we would surrender they would not bring this artillery across Brice's Creek and the swamp. The reply was that he should not surrender, and saluting each other they turned each to join his command. As he came back he saw what he suspected, that the enemy had taken advantage of the truce. As soon as firing ceased, some sixteen hundred men arose from their sheltered positions and came out into sight, and those that had not good positions advanced and took them. Capt. Aigan called Lieut. Durfee and myself together and informed us of the result of the interview, and asked our opinion. We at once endorsed his position; we saw that the capture of the fort was only a question of time, and the only question aside from the lack of water was the right of sacrificing the men. From the advantage the enemy had secured by advancing to new positions in violation of the truce, we saw that we could hardly hope to work the gun, or use the muskets for any length of time. The only course left was to surrender the fort, provided we could get such conditions as we deemed honorable. A white flag was then raised by us, and soon the one that came from the enemy returned. When we saw it approach, Capt. Aigan started out to meet it. The terms of surrender and the manner of their fulfillment, according to the code of Southern honor, shall be the theme of the next paper.

*Zion's Herald and Wesleyan Journal,* November 9, 1864, p. 177.

# ❧ *Letter 3*

Providence, R.I., Nov. 1864

We had two negro cooks in the company, and as Capt. Aigan went out to meet the flag of truce the second time, he told the negroes to look out for themselves if they had a chance. The chance they furnished themselves by slipping through the embrasures and making for the swamp. The rebs discovered them creeping through the brush and gave chase, but the negroes were too fleet for them and escaped into the swamps, and afterwards, reported to Col. Simon of Newbern. Captain Aigan met Col. Falk of Dearing's Brigade of Cavalry under truce,[1] and agreed to surrender the fort on the following conditions:

1. That all private personal property of the officers and men should be respected. This they violated by creeping up and rushing to the quarters of the officers and men and stealing whatever they could get hold of— Capt. Aigan's pocket Bible and all his books and such clothing as they could lay hold of they took. Nor was the plunder confined to the privates; line and staff officers and surgeons all went in together. I had to double up my fist to prevent a staff officer from drawing off my gauntlets. They were prevented from taking off my spurs by my constantly stepping about; my horse was shot in action and they stripped him of all his equipment, etc.

2. They agreed that the regimental chaplain who was present in the performance of his official work should not be treated as a prisoner of war, but be allowed to return to his post. This agreement they violated by treating me in every respect as a combatant, and by keeping me prisoner for nearly five months.

3.   That two negroes who were company cooks should be treated with humanity, and that two children who were near the fort and entered it when the action came on, should be treated as non-combatants. As I intimated above, the negroes did not choose to commit themselves to the tender mercies of high-minded Southrons, but skedaddled for the swamp after the most approved style. The two white men were taken with us to Kinston and put in jail. On our march, one, a native of North Carolina, was recognized and claimed for the army under the conscript act. The other was section master on the railroad, and originally from New York. The rebels said he was a deserter for them, and brought up a number who swore they knew him. I have no doubt they kept their word to release them by thrusting them into their army.

4.   They agreed that the officers should retain their side arms and the fort should be surrendered with the honors of war, the troops marching out with arms and music. They broke this part of the terms of surrender by allowing the officers to retain their side arms till they had marched about one mile from the fort, and then compelled them to give them up. But one thing we were not to be cheated out of, and that was the surrendering the fort with the honors of war. After the soldiers had gathered up what they wanted, or could obtain of their effects, they assembled in the fort. While this was going on I went down in the rifle pit just outside the fort to take a last look at my noble horse, and found that, although severely wounded, he was not dead. He looked at me and moaned piteously. I am sure he knew me. I requested a rebel soldier to put a ball through his head and close his suffering. 'Twas better he should be good for the vultures then bear a rebel, a traitor, an enemy in the seat where a patriot rode. Returning into the fort I saw a rebel attempting to plant the red battle flag on the parapet. I went at once to Col. Falk, and said this fort is not yet surrendered, and requested him to order the flag removed. He ordered it taken away. Before the action commenced the officers' trunks were taken from the quarters into the fort, and although the rebels urged Capt. Aigan and Lieut. Durfee to give them some of the things they could not carry, they insisted on giving what they did not want to their own men. Col. Falk would not allow any violence on the officers, and so our men got the things. When the tents were struck preparing for the action, the tent that was used as the officers' quarters, fell across and covered a large company chest, partly filled with clothing. This escaped the attention

of the enemy, and Capt. Aigan gathered a group of his own men about him, and gave its contents to them.

When we were ready Capt. Aigan gave the order for the men to fall in, and they took their muskets and prepared to evacuate the works. With music, and all the pomp our little handful of nearly fifty men could give, we marched out. Sixteen hundred men, partly mounted, and others on foot, surrounded us. Our good national airs never sounded sweeter to me, and musicians never played better; and alas for some of them, for they were their last tunes. And yet I trust their cunning fingers skilled in loyal service on earth have awakened higher melody in a land where traitors come not, and where a lack of food consigns not the dweller to a painful and lonely death. Proud was the step and lofty the bearing of those Rhode Island men as they marched across the drawbridge to the ground in front where we were to conclude the formalities of the surrender. Saluting with the usual form our national standard, arms were stacked, and the work and garrison surrendered. Firing ceased about half-past two, P.M., and we turned and marched from the fort under guard shortly after four o'clock. When men talk to me of Southern honor I recall the terms of our capitulation, and the method of their violation.

We were marched about one mile along the railroad toward Newbern, where we remained till about sundown. The woods and country about was full of rebels. Some were foraging, some cooking, and others burning the railroad and other property. Here we first came in contact with officers of all grades in a free and easy manner, and without embarrassment entered into a discussion of martial and political affairs. Of course we would stand aloof until invited into a discussion. It usually ran thus: After meeting a confederate officer it would not be too long before, by some remark, he would throw down the gauntlet and invite to discussion. We would answer that he could not expect a reply under the circumstances, and that we were well aware that we were prisoners of war. This would draw from them an invitation to talk with perfect freedom and an assurance of protection. As soon as we could get this we were ready for the fray, and both sides would pitch in for a free fight of talk. Sometimes when the conversations closed, I used to think it imprudent to give such emphatic denunciations to men who were full of fire and armed to the teeth, and would resolve to be more cautious, but when the time came all thoughts of prudence would vanish, and we would denounce them and their treason as freely as in our own tents in the union lines. Sometimes we could hear the bystanders curse and threaten, but no one ever struck or fired on me, although in one or two cases they handled their arms a little careless I thought, and occasionally they would push me a little with the musket. Perhaps my attempt to get full as much liberty as was assigned me had something to do with it.

Just as the sun passed from sight, we were ordered to fall in. Here we saw some of the bloody evidence of the effect of our fire. Some said we killed four and other ten times four. What the actual casualties of the fight were, I do not know. We lost no man.[2] A guard of cavalry took charge of us. The order of the march was for the captain, lieutenant and myself to march in the advance. Then the rebel captain mounted and came behind. After him came the guards, forming a long hollow square, and the men marching in its center. For fear of revolt and conspiracy as they freely told us, we were not allowed to say much to the men. Six miles to Evans' Mill for the first march. The camp fires, the cooking, the songs, the unrest and noise of the horses among the bushes, was like many camp meetings after dark, as the worshipers in social chat sit about the camp fires. As soon as it was known that a Yankee chaplain from New England, and of the Methodist church, was captured, he was sought out as a kind of curiosity and thermometer. First, they seemed desirous to see how a genuine abolitionist looked, and again, they seemed to think that in him they could get at the most recent and radical theory of that to them detested place, New England. On one point my conscience is pretty clear: I think most of the rebs with whom I came in contact think that I not only endorse the emancipation and other kindred falacies, but glory in them. The Adjutant General, as soon as we commenced to march, dismounted, and came and walked with me all the evening.[3] He sought with soft and gracious words to disarm me, and so get at some facts about Newbern, its force, etc. All the light he got out of me he could put in his eye and not blind him. Tired and weary with fighting and marching, we were turned into the old block house, and amid filth and dirt found a place for repose. Of course we got no supper. Among the to me impressive events of that exciting day, I wish to note the following: During a lull in the firing, and while the guns were loading, we all kneeled down around the old flag staff in the center of the fort, and uncovering our heads before God, I offered prayer, seeking the help and protection of the Lord. Would it be presumption in me now to believe that he who ruleth in the heavens and regardeth man, looked upon our humble devotions and remembered us?

Captain Aigan and Lieutenant Durfee with their noble men are yet in the hands of the enemy. Nearly half of their number are already numbered with the noble dead, having suffered the martyrdom of patriot heroes. Peace to the memory of those who will not return to the embraces of their families and the greetings of friends. Ye who mourn the untimely dead look for support and comfort to that God in whom service they have fallen. Those who yet live, by their tears, privations and sufferings, are paying more than the price of blood to save the Union and the dear good flag. I should not be just to the occasion and my privilege, did I omit to mention their bravery and undaunted courage. They all fought well amid the shot and shell, the smoke and confusion of battle. The struggle is now harder in prison than it was in the field. A month's service in the ranks and at the front is easier and more to be desired than one day of prison life among the rebels.

*Zion's Herald and Wesleyan Journal,* November 16, 1864, p. 181.

# ✥ *Letter 4*

Providence, R.I., Nov. 8, 1864

Long and dreary was that first sight of prison life. The only door to the block house was open, and a soldier stood guard before it, and others surrounded it. Snatches of moonlight now and then would steal through the broken clouds. I could not sleep. My thoughts were busy with the new circumstances, and what might come of them. Among the prisoners was one of another regiment and State than mine, whose conduct pained me. He was a copperhead, and went into the service for money. He was thinly clad, as the rebels had taken all his extra clothing, and he could not sleep in the chilly air. Soon he got into conversation with the guard. Worse and more foolishly did he denounce our government than did the rebel himself. He plainly told him he came for money, and that he would never fight the South again. He told of his home, his wife and children. When morning came I got him on one side to talk the matter over. At first he stood it out, and justified himself. The soldiers about were enraged that treason should be justified by one of our own men. "Have you a family?" I said. "A wife and six children at home." "Then," said I, "you ought to be ashamed of yourself for their sakes, if not for your own. When you are dead and gone the course you take will cause them to blush and stammer for your want of manhood to make you stand up before your country's enemies. We know not what may come of our imprisonment, but if you die, die a man, and not a coward and a traitor." We had a long and close conversation. All the men gathered about, and some of us joined the old man's tears as he owned his fault and promised to do so no more. The morning was full of interest. Cavalry, artillery and infantry, with the baggage train, was rapidly moving to the rear.

Among the cavalry I saw a small boy, perhaps twelve or thirteen, riding along. His heavy sword seemed almost mockery as it hung by his side. He was said to be brave. The soldiers were, many of them, young and small. During the morning, one of the servants brought us food. It was on a common breakfast plate, and consisted of scraps of pork rind and pieces of corn bread, gathered from the table of the rebels. Captain Aigan took it, and turning to me, said, "Here, chaplain, take this and give it to the men," refusing to take any himself. I broke the bread into pieces, not so large as my thumb, and gave it out. Not two thirds of the men got even a crumb. I turned to the servant and said, "Go and get these men some food. We fought all day yesterday and marched last night, and are to march to-day, and we need some breakfast." He scraped a little closer and brought us another plate full of smaller pieces. The men joked a little about the generous hospitality of the Southern chivalry, and we fell in, and about nine in the morning marched away. As the column moved we saw the foragers coming from the farm houses with bags full of good things, and sides of bacon strung on poles borne on the shoulders of the soldiers. We saw few fences. The farms were divided by deep ditches, that answered the double purpose of a fence and for draining the land. The pine was the chief timber, and grew to a great size. I heard a man who was conversant with lumber matters say that some of those trees, if in New York, would be worth more than two hundred dollars each for building purposes. For twenty miles back we saw but little evidence of cultivation; the houses were burned and the plantations abandoned. The country is level, sandy, and covered with a dense growth of timber. Large swamps abounding with cedar and cypress surrounded us on every side. The water moves sluggishly, and is of a reddish cast, and has a taste of wood. Wells are found at every house. Some of them were exceeding deep. The white sand looks like a barren, but we soon learned that it was fertile and yielded well. Beneath the skin of sand is clay, and there are indications of marl.

Resting from time to time beneath the trees and beside the brooks, we mingled with the guard, both officers and men, in a free and general conversation. In this we learned that Beauregard was in command, and that between twenty-five and thirty thousand men were in the rebel army that came down to capture Newbern. The reason of their hasty leave was Gen. Butler's advance on Petersburg. Davis ordered him at once to raise the siege, and by a forced march hasten to Kinston, and there take cars for the North. The woods were full of stragglers. The men seemed to feel no obligation to keep in column, but went at such a pace and time as pleased them. The privates seldom noticed or saluted the officers. The discipline seemed to be of the loosest kind. They informed us that they made little pretension to discipline, but said their men would fight just as well. At night the men went where they pleased, and when a fight came on not more than half the men would be in line, but as soon as firing commenced, they would hurry up and go in. If they were absent two or three days no notice was taken of it, they told us, but if a fight came on and they were not present, they were severely punished. Plenty of negroes were in the army in Confederate uniform with muskets in their hands. When we asked if the negroes were not soldiers, they said they were servants to planters' sons, and when on a march carried their arms. The comparative value of the currency of the North and the South was commented upon. By asking the market price of various articles, we found that any given article would cost from twenty to forty times as much in Confederate scrip in the South as in "greenbacks" in the North.

The rapid and continuous firing of our gunboats as they followed us up the river shelling the woods, grew fainter and fainter, and finally died away. The pontoon train was new and in fine order. The horses were in excellent condition. Each cavalry man owns his own horse, and so is interested to take good care of him. A horse costs from three to five thousand dollars, and so if a man loses his horse by his own neglect he must purchase another or go into the infantry. If the horse is shot in action the government furnishes another. The cavalry service is the most popular branch in the Confederate army, and men offer large premiums to get into it.[1] After a weary march of some twenty miles, as an old man informed us, we came on May 6th to Pollocksville, N.C. 'Twas about sundown. We were stationed in a field, and took quarters on the fresh green grass. From the surrounding regiments many officers gathered about us to see, to talk, to trade. Steadily and directly they looked. All sorts of questions. Offers for this and that garment. We were too fresh captives to be willing to trade much. The general custom of stripping prisoners to a partial extent had been omitted in our case. They took only a part. About ten o'clock we were furnished rations. The captives were sixty in number. We drew about three pecks of unsifted corn meal and some bacon. Not two ounces of bacon for a man. No other article was given us. We sent to a camp near and borrowed a skillet, and mixing the meal with water, attempted to make bread. We had no salt. Nearly two hours were consumed in baking ten cakes by the camp fire. We cut each cake into six parts and gave one to each man. The cakes were about eight inches across and an inch and a quarter thick. They were not sufficiently cooked, and I gave mine to a soldier, as two days had not made me hungry. The bacon I ate raw.

Our chance for escape was small, as the guard used the utmost vigilance, and reclining upon the grass we were soon sleeping. We expected to have a chance in the morning to cook the rest of our meal and get a good breakfast, but at a quarter before five we were ordered to fall in, and without breakfast or dinner we were marched forty miles. The men carried the meal for a while, and then threw the bag into a baggage wagon, and we never saw it afterwards. We were urged forward for several miles at almost double quick. There was one extra horse with the guard, and Capt. Martin,[2] who had us in charge, allowed us to take turn in riding. I rode several miles during the day. But this was but a partial relief. The day was one of the warmest I ever saw. We were put in the rear of the artillery train. The wheels of more than one hundred guns, with caisons and attending wagons, cut up the sandy roads, and it was like marching in a newly ploughed field. The officers were kept separate from the privates, and we were ordered to march in front. We had gone on many miles, and the men were showing the effect of the treatment. One cavalry man was weary and tired, and became greatly enraged, and said, "Capt. Martin, give me back my sword and horse and I will fight my way back to Newbern." Drawing his pistol, he swore that another word about fighting would cost his life. When the men began to show symptoms of exhaustion and got behind, the guards would raise their carbines and order them to "close up," as no one alive would be left behind. We all understood that if we could not go on that we would be left in a condition that would give them no further trouble. All did their best. O the horrors of that dreadful march! Deepest of all past suffering has that burned itself into my recollection. Hour after hour went by of the hottest day, mile after mile of that sandy road. Past trees and brooks and fields and the ruins of sacked buildings, we hastened on. We were kept well up to the artillery train. It was forced march. Endurance began to fail. The men began to fall. I appealed to the Captain to allow us to go more slowly. He answered that his orders were imperative to keep up to the train, and he could not violate them. I said the men could not stand it. He replied they must stand it. I said you will kill the men at this rate. He replied that he was sorry for the men, but must obey his orders.

After a time Capt. Aigan and I concluded something must be done or the men would be melted down. We had some personal effects about us. My saddle, blanket and equipments that they took from my horse after they shot him, they agreed to turn over to me, as I was a noncombatant. They were among the spoils in the brigade, but I was not fool enough to suppose I should ever see them again. I might, however, turn them over to Capt. Martin, and by so doing make way for a new appeal for my men. I then approached him and told him it was my wish that he should have my equipment, and handed him my gauntlet and spurs. The other officers also made him a contribution of a field glass, etc. He seemed much pleased. He said he hoped to be promoted and should value them much, especially the saddle, as it was exceedingly hard to obtain one of good pattern. It was a McLellan saddle; and by the way that is just the pattern that pleases the rebels. Whether the man who gave the name of this style of saddle would like to be ridden by the rebels as well as they would like to ride him, I cannot tell. After some more general conversation I made a new appeal to him to go more slowly and spare the men. At first he said he could not, but after a while he began to yield. I appealed to his manhood, the fear of God, the judgment, and told him kindly but plainly, that if he killed our men by hard marching that God would visit it upon him. He at length halted the column and gave them rest and water. From this time our men were frequently halted, and then we pushed on. About 10 o'clock we reached Kinston jail, where we were turned in behind the bars, and the rusty iron door was locked upon us. The artillery train got in some five hours before us. A man acquainted with the course we took said we marched forty miles that day. When the men became so weary that they staggered, some of the guards would give them a ride for a mile, and this helped a good deal, but some of the men did not ride one step. When I had marched fifteen or twenty miles, I seemed almost exhausted, but after that my system seemed almost to lose sensation, and in a kind of numbed torpor I marched mechanically forward. A soldier had a small bundle of clothing with his blanket, and also a coat belonging to Capt. Aigan. A mounted rebel came up and joined our guard, and no one noticed but that he was one of the guard. Presently he said to this soldier who had the largest and best bundle, "Would you like a ride?" He replied that he would. After riding some distance the owner of the horse asked him if he was rested. The soldier dismounted, but at the suggestion of the rebel left his bundle to be carried by the horse. For a time he rode along as if connected with us, and then suddenly was gone into the woods, and we saw him and the clothes no more.

*Zion's Herald and Wesleyan Journal,* November 23, 1864, p. 185.

# *Letter 5*

Providence, R.I., Nov. 10, 1864

From Thursday morning till Saturday night we got into the substance of half a good meal. We fought and marched all the time. We had not been in the Kinston jail long before they brought us hard bread and raw bacon. Dark and filthy was the place, but we were so exhausted that hunger alone kept us awake till we could take some food, and we were soon lost in profound slumber. It was late in the morning of the holy Sabbath before we awoke. Among the first sounds I remember was the scolding of our men. I soon learned that we had been treated to another specimen of Southern nobleness. On retiring, the men put some of their things, such as hats, shoes, coats, etc. in the recesses of the windows. It was warm, and the windows were open. The guards were stationed outside, a few feet from the jail, and so of course no one but those they permitted to approach could come near. They meanly stole these things from the men. Our canteens were of tin, and so large that they could not be drawn through the square formed by the iron bars. The men then were without these articles, as they could not be replaced. Complaint was made to the officers about it, but they did not seem to care. Nothing came back to us. The morning light revealed to us more perfectly the character of our quarters. We were in the space between the cells and outer wall of the jail, a kind of entry and passage way, filthy with dirt, tobacco and refuse matter of the prison; rats, mice, cockroaches, and visitors more minute and annoying. The cells were full of deserters from the rebel army, and political prisoners or Union men who would not be still.

I found here also five deserters from our own lines. Those who go from us are no favorites with them; they trust them worse than any others. So filthy was the place that we appealed to Lieut. Williamson,[1] who had us in charge, to allow us to go out to some house and arrange our toilet, which request he granted. We went with a guard to a house near by, and which was evidently the property of a well-to-do family. They treated us kindly. They were rebels, and no mistake. The carpets were gone, and everything bore marks of the great convulsion that we were more and more to see. There were but few negroes about. Nearly all had gone to the Yanks. There were no men about fit for the military service. Ladies were plenty, pretty and saucy; they understood and made us feel that we were prisoners of war. The army was passing through the town and departing by rail, and many friends who were in the army were constantly calling, and from the ladies received most cordial reception. In the presence of ladies they would scorn to notice or speak to us. Long and mournful was the tale they told of the trials and privations the war had brought; and from what I know myself, I guess some of them have been crowded a little. No conversation runs long with these people before "nigger, nigger" is thrust into the theme; and you must, like a mean craven, silently endorse what they in a dogmatic way announce, or take issue, and in a skirmish of talk fight it out. Some men are too stern and uncompromising in their natures to cower and cringe before error and treason, and so they demean themselves after a style that does not win them many favors; but the men who cringe and creep they look upon as mean dogs. An hour or two of irksome and awkward conversation, and Captain Aigan, Lieutenant Durfee and myself joined our guard, who with musket in hand waited beside the door with his eye constantly upon us, and returned to prison. Kinston is a small inland town, pleasantly located on the Neuse River, and on the Atlantic and North Carolina R.R. Before the war there might have been from one to two thousand inhabitants, but as it is in the region of raids from our forces, some have gone further inland. Small boats can come up the Neuse River to this point and above.

During the morning the privates, a few at a time, were allowed to go to the street pump not far off, to wash. The boys, negroes, and curious of the town, gathered to look upon us as a kind of show. The jeers and insulting remarks were endured as best as we could bear them. A Presbyterian Church was near us, and the bell for service called up in a strange contrast old memories and new circumstances.[2] I asked permission to go to church, but was denied; "Can I go and sit on the steps outside?" "No sir." As the people went and came, I could watch them, but to be denied even to listen was all new to me. I doubt not their service would have pained me, but I felt an intense curiosity to know what they did say among themselves where they had it all their own way. The prison quarters were changed during the day, and we were removed to the Court House, where we had plenty of room. The building had been used for army purposes, and was in a sad plight. Inscriptions and drawings illuminated and adorned the walls. Troops were passing all the day, and no one seemed to stop the movement of troops because of the Sabbath. Towards night I held service among our own men. We sang together in a subdued but hopeful strain. The basis of my remarks was the blessed and hopeful psalm, "The Lord is my Shepherd." Every knee bowed as I offered prayer. Such ability to lay hold of the promises I have seldom felt. Home and loved ones, and dear country, and the sacred flag and its noble defenders, as well as our personal salvation and holiness, were themes that then and there had a new inspiration, and we *worshipped God.* There is more heart in any worship, I think, than is usual in civil life; but with us there were reasons why we should be solemn and tender before the Lord. But we were not dejected. More of song than sorrow. The rebels furnished us no light. On the floor we found our beds, and enjoyed good rest. I found many chances for personal conversation with the men, and so long as we were together I held daily services with them.

On Monday May 9th, I asked the lieutenant who had us in charge to walk out with me. In the Neuse River, just below the town, is the new iron-clad ram that for a long time had been building there.[3] I had a fine chance to inspect it. After it was ready to move, the officer appointed to command her got up steam and started to take her down the river. Of course her trial trip was an event, and all the town was out to see. The whistle was blown, the bell was rung, and with a full head of steam, with the rapid current (for the river was then high) she moved down the Neuse. She drew eight feet of water. The pilot did not know the channel, and supposed he had more water than he had. She had not gone half a mile before she got to the right of the channel, and with full speed ran on a bar of clay and sand, and such was her speed, that she ran her horn forty feet into the bar, where she stuck fast. I did not tell the officer with me so, but I felt a wonderful spirit of resignation to the will of Providence come over me as I saw the nose of that engine of death stuck fast in the mud. She has a sloping roof, with heavy armor of iron plates about 4½ inches thick. Her roof is in fact an eight square oblong turret, covering her guns and machinery. She has two guns, one in each end of the turret; each end of the turret or sloping roof is perforated for the guns, with five ports for each gun. I was informed that her armament was one hundred pound guns, but they did not seem to me to be so large.

Her ports were furnished with iron doors, that are lifted by chains when the gun is run out, and the recoil shuts them. I should judge her to be from a hundred twenty to a hundred and forty feet long. As her horn or ram was under the water, I could not judge how long she was. At that time several large pontoons were being put under her to lighten her up. They hoped to get her so as to go in four feet of water. Her smoke stack is low, and her machinery is under protection of the long roof; her steam pipe is some twenty inches above protection, I should judge, and I thought would make a fine target for a Union gun. At each end of the boat for twenty or thirty feet, the deck is nearly level and free from projections; her large guns effectually command her decks. I did not see any arrangement for sharpshooters, although several could act with advantage from her staircase, which is in the top of the roof or turret, and near the smokestack; her propeller is well down, and so far as I could judge, well protected. She is certainly a strong and formidable boat, and if she was out where she could have a fair chance at our wooden boats, could do much mischief.[4] Report said she was injured when she struck; I asked if she was hurt, and they told me she was not. Several plans were being agitated to float her off and get her into service; one was to dam up the river and so float her. The objection was that it might injure her to attempt to float her before her ram was loose; one was to dig out around her and lighten her.

During the day a Universalist minister, Rev. Hope Bain, hearing that a Yankee chaplain was among the prisoners, called on me.[5] He at once asked me what right we had to come down there to interfere with their negroes. He proceeded to show me, by certain arguments, that the negro was only fit to be a slave, that he was better off *as he was* among the Southern people, that God made him *for that use,* and was rampant and raging at the Yankees for their sacrilegious presumption in attempting to set them free or use them as men. As occasion served I responded to his remarks. Finally he said that men so wicked as we were ought to be damned. "But," said I, "you do not believe there is a hell." "Oh, well" said he, "I mean that they should be condemned." I suppose it was because I was either obtuse or perverse that I failed to become a convert to his opinions. I had no Bible, and as he started to go I asked him if he would give me one. He replied that he had no Bible, but he had the New Testament, and gave me that. I was frequently called out to meet and converse with officers of various grades. These conversations were free and open on both sides. Large numbers of soldiers gathered about and listened to the arguments. We were constantly engaged in conversation on the merits of the war, and I did my best to give them some things to think about. At this time all were full of hope for the Confederacy.

Before my capture I heard of the execution of twenty Union men at Kinston by the rebels.[6] On Feb. 1, we were attacked at Newbern by some fifteen thousand men, and several hundred men were captured from us. Among them were some North Carolinians who had before been conscripted into the rebel service and deserted. They came into our lines and enlisted in our service, being true Union men and in favor of the United States. On being captured they were at once tried by a court martial, and twenty were condemned to be hung. They informed me that the place of execution was near, and I asked permission to go and see it. Capt. Aigan, Lieut. Durfee and myself were taken out to walk, and passed by the place. The gallows were still standing; there were four; they consisted of upright posts some sixteen feet high, I should judge, with a beam across the top. The scaffolds on which the men stood were removed, and only the gallows frames remained. Some of the pieces of rope were dangling from the cross beam where the men were cut down. They died true to the North, and died nobly, like heroes and martyrs as they were. Several of them had families here, and the scenes of parting were touching and solemn. The executions were public, and many came to see. Several ministers were present, and some of the men were baptized before the day of execution. All died in Christian hope, and I doubt not their souls have found peace amid the loyal in the paradise of God. When captured, each one was dressed in the uniform of the United States army. After they were hung everything was removed from their bodies, save a pair of cotton flannel drawers. In the night they were taken up and the drawers removed, and the naked bodies thrown back and covered up without shroud, coffin, or winding sheet. The grave is in the open common near the town, and just at the foot of the gallows. All are in one grave. A rude pile of gravel, without the form of a grave, without headboard or memorial marks the place. But that God who has said, I will repay, has marked the spot, and the resurrection angel watches their sacred dust; and the time will come when Moses and Paul and Luther and Washington from among the glorified martyrs will look these men up, and grasp them to sympathetic and honorable embrace. As I stood mournfully looking upon that rude grave, I desired to fall upon and kiss the dust that was their monument and sarcophagus. O, how will the great day of God reverse the judgments of earth?

*Zion's Herald and Wesleyan Journal,* November 30, 1864, p. 189.

— *Letter 6*

Bennington, Vt., Nov. 14, 1864

While Beauregard's army was hastening to meet at Petersburg the force of Gen. Butler, we were kept at Kinston. As the 22d South Carolina was passing, its chaplain, Rev. Mr. Dill, of the Baptist Church, called on me.[1] Our conversation was long and close. We talked of war and religious things. He seemed to honestly think that slavery was right before God. I think I was the first minister who was an out and out abolitionist that he had ever met. He believed the northerners to be almost barbarians. If God had enemies, and a class of men he *despised,* they were the Yankees. That God was not on their side, and that he would not interfere and give them help to crush the army and people of the North, he seemed not to have the slightest thought. He *believed that God* sent the slaves here to be elevated. I asked him if he did not believe that it was the will of God that each creature, the fly, the toad, the dog, the lion, the negro, the white man, the angels, each in its own sphere, should come at length to its highest and most perfect development. He admitted the statement as God's will. Then I said, "Do you believe that *slavery* can do that for the negro?" He pointed to Africa, and to some model plantations. "Do you allow the slaves to read?" "No." "Dare you cultivate and expand the mind of the negro to the fullest extent of his capacity?" "It would not be safe to do so." "Do you think the Bible teaches that slavery is right?" "I do." "Do you think a high, even and honest development of the human mind on examining the Bible without bias, would see African slavery taught in it?" "Well, sir, I think such a man would see that it is God's will to have slavery."

"Do you think that the slaves, if so cultivated, would see it taught in the Bible to be their duty to remain slaves?" "I do not know as *they* would so read it." "Well, sir, admit for the sake of the argument that God sent the slave here, may there not come a time when slavery shall have done all it can for God's negro, and when slavery must have its hand wrenched of the black man, in order to allow him to attain the highest development and elevation of which he is capable?" "Well, there may come such a time." "Well, how do you know but that time has come?" He admitted that it might be, but did not see it in that light. I asked him of the influence of slavery on the white race. He admitted the corruption and immorality of the slaves and the men of the South. I at once saw that Southern ideas of virtue were totally different from those of the North. We then looked at the subject in another light. I asked him the effect of the dwarfing and repressing process on the value of the negroes as skilled laborers. He said they could not educate them above a certain point, and that the policy of course prevented their employment in the higher departments of industry. Said I, "suppose you take two boys of equal mental, moral and physical qualities, the one white and the other black, and subject them to the training of the two sections, South Carolina and Massachusetts. The negro shall be brought up on one of your model plantations, and by one of your planters, and trained so as to make of him the most valuable slave. *Let the other* be trained under the common school and educational system of Massachusetts. He at twenty-one years can read, write and understand the several branches of a good English education, has read one or more of the languages, and is well posted in history and general literature. The slave can neither read nor write, for slavery prohibits that. Now place the two in the productive field, and put them to the best financial use. The slave is worth from two hundred to four hundred dollars per year. The free man is worth from six hundred to two thousand dollars per year, and many of their class reveal a genius that produces from five to fifty thousand dollars per year through machinery and invention." "Now," I said, "which of these systems as a mere cold financial measure and a developer of wealth, is the more desirable?" He replied that he was not accustomed to look upon it in that light. I then spoke of the vast sinking of capital required by the slave system. If a man wishes to engage in business as a slaveholder, he purchases ten thousand acres of land and a thousand negroes. For the land he pays one hundred thousand dollars, and for the negroes he pays one million of dollars. In a system of free labor the man has his whole eleven hundred thousand dollars to invest in lands, buildings, and machinery, or ships. Thus with an advertisement for which he pays ten dollars, he draws to him his thousand laborers, and each one on an average is worth two slaves. While the conversation was running on in this strain, a large concourse of negroes, soldiers and officers had gathered about, and were most intent listeners. Remarks were often thrust in by the bystanders, both for and against the sentiments I was advancing. Evidently no such talk had been heard about there. For some time I had noticed a fierce looking Major walking nervously up and down near the edge of the listeners. In a few moments he approached and ordered the officer of the guard to disperse the crowd and send me back to prison, and not allow any one to call me out again. When he came to me and gave this order, I remarked that it was all the same to me. If they chose to call me out to try and convert me, that they must be responsible for the talk. Then they kept me more closely than before.

The court-house in which we were confined was near the jail, and when we went out we came close to the prisoners there, so we could speak to them. There were five of my own regiment in the cells who had deserted to the enemy. They could not trust them and put them in close confinement. I understood they were to be put to hard work in their workshops under close guard, probably something like a State's prison. These men felt ashamed and shrunk back from me, and did not care to converse. The prisoners had to do their own cooking, being let out once each day in small squads for that purpose. They had an iron skillet for bread and a tin kettle for soup. Several hundred prisoners were in this jail, and an old building some distance off. Some of the political prisoners were old and venerable men, some of them eighty years of age, and many of them men of wealth. I was also informed that the prisons of the South are full of such men. I found that these things did not meet the approval of many of the soldiers. They did not know how to keep out of the army, and so went on against their own will. Some of them saw the drift of things, but had no power to prevent it. But most all I met at this time were confident of the triumph of the South. The soldiers were exceedingly anxious to get our greenbacks, watches, knives, pocket-books, etc. They would pay us in Confederate money. We could get at this place ten Confederate dollars and one of our money. A good silver watch would bring from two to eight hundred dollars, and a good gold watch would bring as high as from fifteen hundred to two thousand dollars. A plain gold ring would bring twenty-five dollars. A pint of molasses cost us three dollars and fifty cents. One day three of us obtained permission to go to the river for a bath. On our way we stopped at a store where we found a small stock of goods. It was said to be a fine assortment. A one horse wagon would take it all at a load. I bought a cheap tooth brush for five dollars and a small sixpenny cake of soap for five dollars more. Going about the town we saw the yard where the ram was built. At the time we were there they were working on some lighters for the use of the iron ram.

On Wednesday, May the 11th, the army of Beauregard had gone forward, so that transportation could be furnished for the prisoners, and at 8 A.M., we were marched to the depot. As we were embarking for our southern journey, we saw by the side of the train the brass Napoleon that did such good service for us, and which the rebels took with us. Our men hailed it as the face of an old friend. Kinston, the place of the grave of the Union martyrs and the port of the stranded ram, we left, and slowly by rail went to Goldsboro. This is a small town of no special importance, aside from its connection with the railway intercept. There are a few good buildings. The Atlantic and North Carolina and the Wilmington and the Weldon Railroads cross each other at this place. Here I first met a rebel who personally insulted me. One of the sergeants commenced on Captain Aigan and myself. We were in conversation by ourselves. He made some insulting remarks, and knowing that I was a chaplain, asked me the most vulgar and indecent questions about negroes. I would not notice him, and he became furious, swore spitefully, and handled his musket a little careless, I thought. He cooled off, however, at length, seeing we would not give him a good excuse for using the cartridge. The negroes came about with pies to sell, and thinking we might get a palatable morsel, we sent out a dollar for one. It was a crust of about the thickness of pasteboard, filled with sweet potatoe paste. It was not exceedingly tempting, and I sent it to some of the men who proposed to try it. At last accounts the good fellow had failed to find a place for it in his stomach. I would not have you infer, however, that his stomach was particularly crowded with food, for I think I remember that no one of our party about that time complained of the gout. The young boys that came to see us were an uncombed and ragged crowd, saucy and bold. We remained here a few hours, and began to see specimens of the natives. The men were all soldiers. The women showed the prevalence of caste. Some dressed richly, but most were dressed in the most untidy manner. Many of them had a stick protruding from the mouth several inches. These persons were chewing snuff. A stick of some kind is taken, perhaps six inches long, and pounded or chewed till it becomes splintered like a broom. This they roll in the snuff till it is full, when they place it between the cheek and the teeth, and suck it with great apparent relish. The negroes were all about, and did not seem to me to be so very much below the common whites that were to be seen on the cars and at all the places we visited.

*Zion's Herald and Wesleyan Journal,* December 7, 1864, p. 193.

# ✑ *Letter 7*

Newbern, N.C., Nov. 22, 1864

Leaving Goldsboro, N.C., we proceeded south on the Wilmington and Weldon Railroad, reaching Wilmington just before dark, May 11th. We had our rations of hard bread and raw bacon, but it did not, somehow, produce just the right impression on the inner man, and we thought to get something better. We knew that the blockade runners came in here pretty freely, and hoped to get a good lunch at least. Asking the lieutenant for permission to go for supper, he sent us under guard to the restaurant in the depot close by. We asked if we could get supper, and were informed we could. Here we met an officer from South Carolina, and another, a renegade Yankee traitor from Connecticut, and a woman that embraced the excellence of both. The Connecticut copperhead, that by legitimate transformation had turned up in the army of Jeff, had not much to say. He smiled complacently on all that the South Carolinian said. We found that several blockade runners had just come in. One brought eleven hundred thousand pounds of bacon, and others brought various stores, and of course they were jubilant and hopeful. The South would win. A free conversation of the merits of the war, and of course terminating in a discussion of the negro question, went on for an hour or more. Several negroes stood about the table, or were peeping in at the doors, and heard all.

The South Carolinian accused us of the North of being favorable to the negro, of seeking to free him from slavery, etc. When the thing came out strongly, we affirmed our purpose to free the negroes, the eyes of the dusky bystander would snap, and their very frames seemed to shiver with a quiet but exultant joy. I think no poor captives have had more attention than those servants bestowed on us. But I would not mislead you to concluding that our fare was much beyond that of Parker's or the Astor House. Some poor ham, good eggs, slop coffee, and bread such as they make "down souf." We did it the most honorable and ample justice. Poor souls. How could we tell the penalty for indulging? Some greenbacks had been converted into marketable Southern goods at the rate of one dollar United States for ten dollars of Jeff's bogus currency. The South Carolinian evidently enjoyed our confusion as we parted with our Southern script, and then in greenbacks made up the value of sixty-five dollars of Confederate money for three inferior suppers, and for which in the North one dollar would have been an ample sum. But this experience at once cured and broke us, for we never again had the presumption to ask to be fed at any special table.

Returning to our company we found many had gone to bed, and the bed all ready for the others. The Southern Confederacy has a very fine variety of beds for her prisoners of war. There is the common floor, the ground under a shed, the sidewalk paved with brick, the sidewalk paved with large flat stones, the street trodden hard, the street paved with paving stones, the meadow or pasture covered with turf, and the soft sand or ploughed field, and sometimes a loose board or a fugitive door. The one we had this night was the best I had seen. A small tract of sand, *clean* sand, was near the depot, and we found it delightful. The benefit of such a bed is at once evident. You, by a few well directed wiggles work yourself down into it, and it fits you like a glove. A paved street, or a brick sidewalk would not fit around the body so well. I have known people to scold and take on because the servants (stupid creatures) did not make up the beds just so. What an amount of trouble such people would escape if they only were boarding down South. Then I have known people to get up from bed to look at the stars and the moon. We could do that without getting out of bed at all. Then to have to go to the window, roll up the curtain, throw up the sash, unfasten and throw open the blind and put out the hand just to see if it is raised. Why, we could find that out in a moment, and keep snug in bed and have our arms folded all the time.

We could not see much of Wilmington, as the railroad is lower than the bulk of the town. There are some fine buildings, and not far from the railroad we saw large embankments of sand; but their nature, whether for military purpose or otherwise I could not learn. The depot is a fine substantial brick structure. About midnight we were ordered to fall in, and crossed the Cape Fear River on a steam ferry boat. Here we met large numbers of troops from Charleston hastening north toward Richmond. They were turbulent, saucy, ragged and homely. Here I saw much cotton. Also we saw the effects of the great fire that broke out at the place a few days before, and just after the Plymouth prisoners passed through on their way South. Jeff. Davis offered fifty thousand dollars reward to find out who set the fire, but no one would tell, although it is pretty well understood that "somebody" did it. Here we were thrust into baggage cars so thick that we could not lay down, and on the Wilmington and Marietta Railroad departed for Florence. The locomotives were old and rusty. The cars had been broken and patched. The rails were worn and poor. We could not go ten miles an hour. Our train broke down and detained us several hours. At length we got under way and came upon a train that had broken down, and that kept us back.

Florence is not a place of importance in itself, and apart from its railroad importance will get its chief interest from being the place where most of the privates of our army that are prisoners of war are kept. Making no delay at Florence, we continued our journey to Kingsville. The old rickety cars, in spite of all their care, smashed up again, and it took us ten hours to gather up the fragments and get under way again. During my ride along this section I had a severe attack of chills and fever. These are quite uncongenial amid comforts and remedies. The shaking and creaking of those rickety cars increased the discomfort. From Kingsville we passed on to Branchville, on the South Carolina Railroad running from Charleston to Atlanta, Ga., and on this went west to Hamburgh, on the Savannah River. Crossing the river we entered the fine town of Augusta.

The Savannah is a large and noble stream at this point, and navigable. I noticed only one or two steamers in the river. Immense cotton storehouses are here, and we saw plenty of cotton. The railroad bridge is well up from the water, and a noble structure. The banks of the river are high on each side of the stream. We left the cars at the river, and marched through the town. The streets are wide, and the town seems well laid out. The land is level. The houses are fine, and many are really elegant. The yards are ample and parklike, and the shrubbery is abundant and charming. The men are few and old. The ladies were numerous, elegant, curious and saucy. The children were impudent, ill bred, ignorant, ragged and dirty. "There go the Yanks," "O, see the blue bellies," "Say, Yanks, where did you come from," "Where you going Yanks?" Profane and vile epithets were mingled after the Southern model. The negroes looked on with a quiet and solemn look. Not a word or act from any negro gave the slightest inclination of joy at our misfortunes.

We remained here only a few hours. The country in all this region I judge to be fine. The land is good. The climate is genial and quite healthy. A Marylander is provost marshall at Augusta. I found any quantity of such men in the South, but they get in as quartermasters, or some safe position. They do not go under fire. From Augusta we went to Millen, on the Central Georgia Railroad, and thence west to Macon. This road was in the best condition of any I saw in the South. The locomotives and cars were in the best state of preservation, and the track was in the best repair. One reason probably is, it has been less used for military purposes, and then they had a better repair shop, I was informed. As we traveled night and day it was an object to get into box cars when we could, if they would not crowd us too much. In the passenger cars we could not lay down. The seats were old and the trimmings gone, making them uncomfortable. The whole floor would be clear in a box car. These cars were used to transport cattle, bacon, soldiers, etc. I think they were not cleaned much. Grease and filth were bad enough; creeping things and the odor of cattle added somewhat to the variety.

Through the country of pines I saw vast quantities of rosin going to waste. In some places I saw hundreds and thousands of barrels stacked up in the open air. The hoops had broken away, the staves fallen down, and the rosin remained standing in columns. As the sun shone upon it, it looked clear and nice. We used to think that the speculators would laugh to get at the cotton and rosin stored and going to waste. We remained at Macon but a short time as we went west, although the officers soon returned there. Leaving Macon in the morning, we went sixty miles to the southwest, to that famous and ever to be remembered Andersonville. On the map it is marked Americus. What I saw and know of that infamous and horrible place, I will speak of in my next.

*Zion's Herald and Wesleyan Journal,* December 21, 1864, p. 201.

# ❧ *Letter 8*

Newbern, N.C., Nov. 24, 1864

Andersonville is a station on the Southwestern and Georgia Railroad, sixty miles to the southwest of Macon, Ga. There is no town or settlement of the least importance. A small wooden church, never completed, and less than a dozen houses in sight. I arrived here at 1½ P.M., Saturday, May 14. We were sixty in the company. Of the Fifth R.I. there were of Co. A, fifty men, with Capt. John Aigan and Lieut. Wm. H. Durfee, and myself. The others were a few pickets picked up at different times. Immediately on our arrival we were ordered out of the cars and formed in line, and turned over to the commandant of the prison. Here I saw that long to be remembered scamp, Capt. Wurtz who was in charge of the Union prisoners of war at that post. He is a lean, tall, rough, coarse looking German. He swears incessantly, and curses most cruelly. While the men were being turned over to him he began to curse them. A cold chill ran over me when I thought that he was to have command and control of our men.[1] The captain, lieutenant and myself he would not receive, and we were sent to the church near by, and remained with the guard that came with us. The men were marched down toward the stockade, a short distance from the depot and in clear view, and I saw them to speak to them no more. It was a sad farewell. But at that time we did not know much about prison life, and all were in pretty good heart.

On our arrival at the church I requested permission to go to some water near by and bathe myself. When at Kinston I bought a toothbrush for five dollars, and small cake of soap for five dollars more, and my long, dusty, dreary ride made me feel like putting them in use. We were put in charge of two soldiers, who went with us to a small stream south of the church, running eastward through a swamp grown up with brush and small trees. Here we were allowed our own time for our bath by the guard. During our journey we made friends of some of the guards, and they did for us all they could. On our return, we went down along the stream toward the railroad, and found several barrels sunk beside the stream full of water for the use of the rebel soldiers. Everywhere I saw the rebels bathing and washing clothes in the brook. The stream ran down toward the railroad and disappeared through a bridge beneath the track.

We returned to our prison quarters at the church, and here met an old looking man mending shoes. He wore a faded and well worn Union uniform. Although he appeared old he was not more than thirty years of age. He had been sick in the rebel hospital, and being nearly dead, was paroled outside the stockade, and being a shoemaker, was furnished with tools and better rations and set to work. He was but a skeleton, and yet deemed himself well compared with what he had been. He told us of the treatment our men received. Soon another of the paroled men came to see us. He was detailed to write, and help in the office of the hospital. At that time there were from ten to fifteen thousand men in the prison. Obtaining permission to take a walk toward the stockade, we went with a small guard and one of our privates for a pilot, across the railroad toward the prison. Crossing a small stream we proceeded to the right, to a position on a hill near the cook-house and between the artillery planted here to command the camp, and the stockade.

It was nearly night. A detachment of rebel soldiers on our left were just having dress parade. A number of ladies were present, and with several officers seemed to be having a fine time. As the stockade ran down the hill and across the stream and up the hill on the other side, I had a good opportunity to see a large part of the grounds within the prison. The size of the enclosure was about sixteen acres.[2] The stockade fence was of wood, and some sixteen feet high, firmly built, with sentry boxes built on the outside, and near the top of the fence. Here soldiers were constantly on guard. The dead line is a small fence running around within the enclosure some twelve feet from the stockade fence. This dead line is a dead line, as many a poor fellow found. The orders were, that if any one put his hand on it, or attempted to pass it, he was instantly shot. Or if a sentinel thought a man was going to attempt to pass it he could fire. The stream of water in which I had my bath I now saw ran down beneath a bridge in the railroad, and through three regiments of rebel guards encamped upon it, into the stockade for the use of our men. Any man acquainted with the way troops use water will at once see what must have been the condition of this water when it entered the prison to our men. When I bathed in it I did not know that it was the stream out of which our noble men must drink or go without; had I known it I would have gone without a bath till this day before I would have touched it. God, I trust, has forgiven me for this unintentional outrage on all human decency, and those noble soldiers I am sure would, did they know my ignorance at the time and the sorrow I have felt since; but how can they, and how should they feel toward those scamps who send the filth of camps and skins into the water for prisoners to drink? The enormity of this indecency is the more glaring when we remember that the stream is very small, a mere brook. Wells were dug afterward, but at this time there were none.

I stood and looked a long time upon the wonder before me. There was not a tree for shade, not a building or tent in the prison. There were all the rude contrivances that the men could arrange for shelter from the heat of the sun, the chill of the night, and the rain. Some made an awning of their blankets. There were few, I should judge not fifty in all. Some got brush and sticks and made a rude roof, and covered it with the clay of which the land is composed. Others dug down and burrowed beneath the surface. Only here and there one of the dense mass could find shelter in this way, and so they had to walk or sit on the ground in the sun, rain and cold. Some had pretty good clothing; some were poorly clad, and some almost naked. Like a vast anthill the multitude went to and fro. Haggard, ragged and hopeless did they seem. This young man who was our pilot, and had been at Richmond and for a long time in this prison, stood and told me things that he had seen till my blood boiled with an indescribable rage and indignation. One day one of our men went down to the brook to wash the only shirt he had. He obtained permission of the guard to hang it out on the dead line to dry. When he came to get it another man was on guard. He had on his person only a pair of old pantaloons, and being weak from a want of suitable food, stood well back and reached out his hand to take his shirt. He lost his balance and fell down, and as it was on descending ground he rolled just under the dead line, and as his body came under the dead line, a ball from the musket of the guard passed through him and ended his sufferings, for in a moment the martyr was dead! Sometimes the men would get so low and discouraged and deranged that they would wish to die, and would call on the guards to shoot them. If they would not shoot, they would pass the dead line, and in a moment their sufferings would be over.

The food they had was corn bread and bacon. The meal was of a coarse kind, made from corn and cobs ground up together and unsifted. This was put in a large trough and mixed with water. No salt was used. This dough was put in pans and baked a little, and then in small pieces issued to the men. The bacon was poor, and often rotten. This was boiled, and in small quantities issued with the corn bread. The cooking arrangements were hardly able to supply food for the number then present, and as the number was increased to between thirty and forty thousand, the cooking arrangements were not enlarged. What food could be cooked was prepared, and the rest issued to the men raw. As no cooking utensils were provided, they had to do the best they could. Sometimes they were allowed to go out after wood, and often they had to go without. The men would, if they got a chance, attempt to escape; but if they were not shot by the guards, the bloodhounds, of which a large number were kept there for the purpose, would chase them down and half kill them as they tore their flesh. The stream of water gradually spread itself out, and disappeared in a swamp on the lower side of the enclosure. The only sink provided was this swampy place, and as there was no means of removing the filth, it came at length to be alive with vermin, and caused a stench past description or conception. As the men would wade into this sea of death their oaths and curses were of the most heart-rending character.

While we were here Capt. Wurtz saw us and came out where we were, and in great rage asked what we were doing there, and cursed us to hell a hundred times, and ordered us to leave and never come round there again. The young man with us moved off when he first saw him, and we went back to our quarters.

*Zion's Herald and Wesleyan Journal,* January 4, 1865, p. 1.

# ❧ *Letter 9*

Roanoke Island, N.C., Nov. 25, 1864

From our quarters, the hum and roar of the prison camp in the terrible and memorable Andersonville came plainly to our ears, like the low murmur of the waves of the sea. After our reconnaisance, in which we got a good view of the whole camp, and from which we were so rudely driven by Capt. Wurtz, we soon put ourselves again in communication with our own men, of which some two hundred were at the time doing various duties outside the stockade. Cannon were planted so as to command the camp from four points. Experienced artillerists were placed to work and man the guns, and at any commotion the men were warned they would open upon them.

Most of our men were sick. The corn meal and corn bread did not agree with our men, and their systems soon became impaired and diarrhea would set in, and they would grow weaker and weaker and finally die almost without a pain. Often a man would get up and walk down to the brook and get a drink and return and lie down, and in a few minutes be dead. In some instances men would be walking along in conversation, when one would fall and instantly expire. When the rations were issued, those men that were so weak would get none, and so the frail would have no chance for life, and would soon be gone. No one was taken to the hospital so long as he could walk, and so great numbers died without being taken there at all. The hospital consisted of a number of small tents, pitched outside the stockade. There were no bunks, beds, or blankets, but the men were laid upon the ground. The medicines were few and poor, and what they had did but little good for want of proper nourishment and care. From forty to eighty men were dying each day, and the mortality afterward increased to as high as nearly two hundred per day.[1] So numerous was [*sic*] the dead that often the burial detail would get behind, and a hundred men would remain over till the next day. At first coffins were used, but as the number of deaths increased, they abandoned the use of coffins and buried them one hundred in a grave. A trench was dug eight feet wide, three feet deep, and long enough to lay a hundred men side by side. Another trench was then dug through the center of this one, six feet wide and some twenty inches deep. The corpses were then placed in this grave, side by side, heads all one way, and then planks were laid on the abutments running through each side of the trench. Brush was then thrown in, and the hole covered with dirt. In some instances only fifty were put in a grave. As soon as any man would die, our men would remove what clothing he had to use themselves, as it was thought wrong to bury men with clothing on, when others were nearly or quite naked.

Prison life makes men hard towards other men. Some it hardens in heart toward God, and others are made tender and thoughtful. Among the prisoners were some bad men, and about three hundred of the worst banded themselves together, and were called the danites, and other called them the raiders.[2] They had men on the watch all the time, and were armed with clubs and knives. When a new company of prisoners came, they would be watched to see what they had, and where they went, and then at night these men would make a raid upon them, and get what they chose to take. If resistance was made, the raiders would make short work with the victim, by murdering him on the spot. Just before I was there, the Plymouth men, some two thousand, strong and well, were put in the prison. Hearing how things went, they prepared themselves, and when the raiders came, they fell upon them and gave them a most excellent beating.

I had a great desire to get inside the prison and to preach to the men. I obtained permission to visit Col. Pearsons [*sic*], commanding the post.[3] I had a long and pleasant interview with him. He seemed willing to allow me to preach, and if Capt. Wurtz did not object, promised to allow me to do so. Capt. Wurtz objected, and I was not allowed in the name of Jesus Christ to offer a few words of sympathy to our abused men. I felt I could not have it so, and appealed to the surgeon, but I could not prevail. O how my soul longed to preach Christ to those dear and dying men.

You remember how large and liberal were the supplies sent to the Sanitary

Commission, and by friends to the prisoners at Libby Prison, Richmond, last winter; you also remember the complaints made by our officers that the rebels stole much, and gave them but little. Our men told us that two hundred and seventy-five of these boxes were brought down to Andersonville for the use of the officers and the garrison. Our informant was a good and truthful man, and was employed in a position to know, as the contents of the boxes were used to supply the table at which he ate, after the officers had finished. He said he thought we had as good a right to it as any one, and so brought us coffee, sugar, bread, and a cake of fine soap sent by some northern wife or mother, to husband or son in prison.

I visited Dr. Johnson and asked him many questions about our men.[4] Their want and destitution he admitted, and also said that they were unable to give them what was needed for their health. He said if stores were sent him he would see that they were faithfully distributed. The use made of the boxes in their hands at that time did not exactly look like doing all that honest-minded men could do for our men. As I was at the depot on the day of our departure for Macon with Capt. Aigan and Lieut. Durfee, the sun came down upon us on the platform so intensely, that I asked permission to go into the commissary building, that was part of the long building used for railroad and other purposes. The men that were issuing rations allowed us to come in, and we sat down upon some sacks quite out of the way.

It was the holy Sabbath, but it made no difference to the rebels. The railway trains run the same as on other days, and are more used. Rations were issued, and all camp and garrison work went on as usual. Presently the officer in command came in and saw us there, and with rude oaths drove us brutally out. Even the officers in charge of us was annoyed, and took us round the building so as to allow us to sit in the shade. I saw a short distance from where I was a large heap of boxes. I arose and sauntered out toward them, and found them to be the identical ones described to me by the Union soldiers. They were all sizes, from twelve to twenty inches square, and even larger. They had on them the red labels and prints of the northern express companies. They were directed with paint to colonels, majors, captains, and lieutenants, *Libby Prison, Richmond, Va.* Half of them were out doors, and the rest in a storeroom of the building. Many of the boxes were empty. Others seemed not to be opened as yet. Some were opened and examined, and the contents found spoiled, and the box was left opened and partly emptied. In the room and on the ground, the rubbish from these boxes, consisting of loaves of mouldy bread, cords of biscuits and loaves of cake, cooked fowls, hams, all kinds of rotten fruit, dried fruit, all covered with mould; papers of flour, sugar, and garments spoiled by being in contact with things that had spoiled in consequence of not being delivered promptly, was nearly knee deep. The glass was broken in the window through which I saw the ruin in the room. Nice woolen shirts, such as are called sutlers' shirts, (being usually supplied by sutlers,) coats, pants, hats and caps, and shoes, taken from these boxes, were on the persons of commissary and quarter masters' sergeants, and those employed about the depot.

So near as I could judge, no attempt was made to stop or conceal the plunder.[5] This wholesale and shameful stealing I had read and heard about, but it seemed far off, and I thought perhaps it might be a little overstated; but when I came to look upon it with my own eyes, in broad day, and to hear of it from those who saw the whole thing, and then to see just before my face thousands of noble men reeling and staggering to a starved man's grave for the want of some of these very things, how could I help cursing that hellish and unearthly Confederacy, in the name of my God. But at that time my observation was small, my experience limited, and my emotions were comparatively calm. I was to see and feel more of that iron that for scores and scores of years the slaveholders of the South have been thrusting into the souls of the children of God. Experience initiates us into a conception of their sorrows, and a sympathy for the crushed and bleeding. White men now are beginning to tell a tale of sorrow, akin to that which for ages, from the abused and dusky chattels of these Southern States has been poured into the ear of God.

*Zion's Herald and Wesleyan Journal,* January 18, 1865, p. 9.

# ❧ *Letter 10*

Newbern, N.C., Dec. 15, 1864

Strange are the anomolies that human character furnishes. No stranger event has fallen under my observation than the one I am about to relate. The officers of the three regiments of guards and the officers of the prison had joined and gathered up a grand ball.[1] I should as soon think of having a band of negro minstrels perform the funeral service of a bishop. Men in that Andersonville stockade were starving and dying in their hands, and under their treatment, by the score and hundred, and yet they could gather the ladies of the whole region, obtain a band, and have a drunken revel. For intimations thrown out, I judge that spirits infernal, as well as those of apple brandy and whisky, got into the performances of that saintly set. I saw plenty of those amiable damsels, and have felt that peculiar class of emotions that are awakened when they cast upon those charming secession glances so often spoken about but never described. The fact is, my dear doctor, God in the munificent wealth of his own wisdom has seen fit to create several classes of creatures, and the exact use to which some of them should be put is to some of us not quite so clear. But races have appeareed and gone; American slaveholders were and are. In a little, history will be the museum in which will be stored the relics of an effete and departed tribe. God give them speedy passage to that oblivion that must cover them ere this nation can have rest. Such was my prayer; so pray I yet.

The ladies that danced I presume were all white, but many of the dusky shades, and of several varieties, were all about us. The band was composed of negroes that were by no means black. They played well. The Andersonville prison, or, as the men call it, the "slaughter pen," seems to be looked upon by the Southern women as a kind of grand show, and on Saabbaths the trains from each direction come loaded down with the curious and the scoffer. They come and gather on the high grounds that overlook the stockade, and watch the inmates. The rebel soldiers join them in the jolly walks. Outside all was life, sport, laughter and joy. Inside all was gloom, sadness, insanity, starvation and death. Calmly and coldly, I watched every move, and listened to every joke and jeer. So huge and deep suffering, so sharply thrust upon so large a number for so long a time, and so squarely and unblushingly endorsed, never was on the face of this earth, and when slavery is gone will never be again, for all other institutions will be utterly unable to produce a race of scoundrels capable of such unearthly crime.

Before leaving I saw the commandant of the prison and asked him if he would allow me to go inside and remain for the summer with the men. He said they could furnish their own chaplains. Among the prisoners are a few negroes, and several officers of negro regiments; one major, whose name I have forgotten, and some others. Occasionally a few letters are taken in and delivered to the prisoners, and they pretend to send those the prisoners write. As a general thing, however, I think they are never sent away at all, especially those to go outside the Confederacy lines. The rule for writing was to use a half sheet and write on one page. If it was written on both sides, or between the lines, it would not be sent. When letters came to the prisoners there would often be ten cents due on them; if the prisoners had no ten cents the letter would be taken back and kept from him. Some of the men who had not heard from home in a year or more would come to get their letter, and not having the money would go almost crazy to get it, but the tears and supplications would do no good.

At first they had old troops to do guard duty about the stockade, but after a time they were removed, and the State troops, "the new issue," as they were called, took their place. Our men fared worse then. The raw troops were boys and infirm and old men, and they were harsh and hard. The boys especially thought it a great thing to shoot a Yankee. I think such were rewarded by promotion, or a furlough.

The country about was rolling and uneven, well wooded and I think generally healthy. The location had nothing to do with the sickness of the men. The cause of the suffering were too small quarters, no shelter, no beds, poor food poorly cooked, and not enough of it, and often entirely raw, the want of suitable clothing, water and exercise, the lack of all news from home, and the reign of terror under which they were compelled to live. The heat of the sun and the cold chilly air of the night, with the drenching rains, our men not used to them, could not fail to break them down. The sun scorches and burns like a furnace. A cold chill begins to creep over one at dusk, growing colder, till from one till four in the morning, when it is almost as cold as in a northern winter. Of course it is not so cold; but with a warm blanket and thick overcoat over me I suffered with cold as severely as I ever did in the frost and snow of the North. The burning sun unfits the system to endure cold. The chilling nights that I met in the highlands of Georgia, at Andersonville and Macon, for these are called highlands by Southerners as distinguished from the low and swampy regions of the coast, I did not find at Savannah, Ga., or Charleston, S.C. The night on the coast I found to be of the mildest and most delightful character. But, O, Andersonville, thy memory stings me as the remorse of crime stings a penitent. Perhaps you will tire of this detail about this Confederate war prison, but the wan-faced children of hunger keep coming up before me asking a plea for their woes, and I can hardly break from the subject.

At 11 o'clock, Sunday, May 15, we were ordered aboard the train, and in company with soldiers and women we started for the officers' prison of Macon, sixty miles from Andersonville. The officers and privates were kept well apart, and hardly any communication was allowed between them. Occasionally a letter got through, but we were not allowed to visit them. The reason was obvious. It would not be safe. They feared a conspiracy. Once loose and under leaders, from fifteen to forty thousand men would disorganize the whole region. Also they knew that if the abused and indignant men were once out, that their revenge would be cruel, vindictive, and indiscriminate.

My position with my brother officers was on the rear platform of the last car in the train. The cars were crowded, and we chose this position for the opportunity it gave to study the country, people, buildings, crops, etc. The stores at the cross roads were everywhere abandoned. We seldom saw a man who was not a soldier. Negroes and women were numerous. The only things growing were corn, with army beans planted between the hills of corn. The amount of land under cultivation, compared with the fields lying waste and growing up to weeds and brush, was small. There was no cotton growing. The chief fruit was the peach. Some of these

47

orchards are several miles long, and as wide as we could see. The fruit is much inferior, both in size and quality, to the New Jersey fruit. Through all this region the soil is quite good for agricultural purposes. On the banks of the brooks and rivers, and wherever the railroad ran through a cut, we could see variagated clay banks almost precisely like the formation at Gay Head, on Martha's Vineyard. Nearly every color, and of the deepest tints, were shown in these gaily colored banks. It is almost as firm as rock, and does not cave, and washes but slowly. The wells are all dug through it, and they need no walls but the simple clay. I have seen these wells that had been in use for years, and yet the sides were as round and smooth and firm as though they had been cut in solid granite. Wild hogs and cattle were to be seen here and there roaming at will through the forests. The cleared lands embrace but a small fraction of the country. The timber in Western Georgia is much inferior to that on the Atlantic coast. The buildings are small, and of the usual inferior character of those occupied by the Southern people.

In the large towns there are some good buildings, and occasionally we see a fine house, but you would not see one once in ten miles in the country. You look on the map and you will see the names of towns all along the railroads, but there are not half of these towns that have five long-houses apiece, in sight of the water tank and wood yard. The locomotives all burn wood, and you will see several slaves at each station preparing the wood, which is done with the axe. The water is pumped up into the tanks by mules, with a rude gearing prepared for the purpose. The negroes seemed to be the property of the railroad corporation. Gangs of negroes were all along the tracks, carefully collecting and burning all stumps, brush, and old ties and sleepers, and whatever was combustible. We interpreted it to be a wise precaution on the part of Jeff. to remove whatever would help the raiders to destroy the track. All the movements seemed to show that the minds of the leaders were full of apprehension.

*Zion's Herald and Wesleyan Journal,* February 1, 1865, p. 17.

# *Letter 11*

Newbern, N.C., Dec. 7, 1864

As we left Andersonville we met a gentleman, a well-bred gentleman.
I mention it, because in my recollection it stands almost alone. He did
not insult us, did not reproach us, did not thrust the negro in our faces,
and denounce us if we refused to say "yea" to his assertions that "God
made him to be a slave, and that it would be a sin to let him go free."
He was a young student in one of the military schools, and out on some
temporary duty connected with the government. He had traveled extensively
in the North, and seen men and places. He conversed easily and freely.
Sitting down on the platform of the car, he made one of our party and
spoke of the men he had seen, of our schools, and the various things of
note, as though there was no war. The uniforms of the Southern soldiers
consisted of a gray jacket and pantaloons, and usually a cap of the same
material. The buttons were of wood, but as fast as they could get hold
of our brass buttons, they cut off their own and substituted ours. Some
of the Southern States have a State button, but they seem to have only
a limited quantity of them. The buttons used by our officers were worth
five dollars each, Confederate money. The cloth was made almost entirely
of cotton. The Southern soldier has no knapsack, as a general thing, but
constantly carries on his person a cotton haversack. Some have blankets
of an inferior quality, some have bed-quilts, and some a strip of carpet;
but many have nothing of the kind. They were constantly asking us to
sell whatever we chanced to have. Canteens were worth from six to ten
dollars, Confederate money. They cost us some thirty cents. Some of our

men would not sell. The guard refused to allow us to go and fill our canteens with water, and so one of the rebel soldiers was ordered to fill them for us. I have a very vivid recollection of the method adopted by one to get a good haul of plunder. Taking a half dozen to fill at the well, he somehow got delayed, and the train went on and left him. The next train of course would bring him; but so far as we were concerned, the canteens had "gone up." The women we saw on the cars were poorly, and not very tastefully dressed. Perhaps I ought to add that a common calico dress cost one hundred dollars. But they do get crinoline; where from, and of what quality and style deponent [witness] saith not.

It was late in the afternoon when we reached Macon.[1] A group of small boys surrounded us as under guard we were marched to our prison. Macon is a fine town, situated on a somewhat elevated position, and has several good buildings. Several schools, and some government works of importance are here; an arsenal and some gun works in which have been placed the machinery taken from Harper's Ferry. The depot and repair shops are fine buildings. Our place of confinement was the Fair Ground, a mile or so from the town.[2] Since the war these grounds have been used for military purposes; sometimes as a camp for their own troops, and then for a prison for United States soldiers. The grounds were originally surrounded by a picket fence, but the fortunes of war have made sad gaps in it, as almost everything you see in the South. On the 20th of April, some fifteen days before our capture, Plymouth, N.C., after a desperate fight of several days, surrendered to the enemy. Some two thousand of the men were at Andersonville; one hundred and thirty of their officers were at Macon.[3] We were placed among them. A few days before the rebels had performed on them that peculiar and characteristic operation denominated "going through them"; that is, they come upon them with speed and enthusiasm, and, with several suggestive and, peculiar, epithets, pick from pockets, head or foot whatever they may chance to desire. The Union officers thought it would be a good joke to come down on us, and so in mock earnestness they surrounded us, and for a time I thought we were to be stripped, sure enough.

The camp at that time was in an open field, and guards were placed about to keep our men together. When we were seen coming, the cry was raised, "Fresh fish, fresh fish," and the whole camp at once turned out, and came down to the point where we were to be turned in.[4] I shall never forget the pain I felt as the mock raid was made upon us. "Come out of that hat"; "Come out of those good boots"; "Here, give us your money"; "Tom, go take that man's blanket"; "Come out of those pants." In a few moments we discovered the thing was all a joke, and intended as a burlesque of the Confederate officers and soldiers. It seemed a little rough at first; but we soon saw through it all, and joined in the laugh. The stockade was not finished, and all was confusion among the rebels incident to the founding of a new prison, and by some oversight Capt. Aigan, Lieut. Durfee and myself were not searched. The almost universal custom of "going through" a man when captured, and again at the provost marshall's office, and also when turned into prison, fortunately for us, was forgotten. Among the officers, we found several that we knew. They all received us with great kindness and were eager for the latest news. What was said about their capture, and who reported dead, and if they were blamed in the papers, what is Grant doing, what news from Sherman, what was gold worth, etc. etc. indicates the kind of information sought. The rebels had given our officers some good tents, and they were quite comfortable. The brigade had just been paid off, and there was a great deal of Union money, or "greenbacks" as our currency is universally called, among our officers. We used to get from four to ten dollars, Confederate money, for one of ours. They had the old and new issue. The new issue was dated 1864, and passed at par. The old issue embraced previous dates, and was much inferior in appearance to the new, and was passed at one third discount. The exchange was conducted on the sly. The rebel government was seeking to stop the circulation of greenbacks among the people, and the most stringent regulations were adopted, and so far as could be, enforced. No rebel before another would purchase our money, but alone each would purchase. Officers and men were in speculation. Afterwards, however, regulations were adopted enabling us through the commandant of the prison to exchange, and of the tricks and lies I shall have much occasion to speak; but I must not anticipate.

Rev. Charles Dixon, Chaplain of the 16th Conn. Regt., a local preacher of our church, and a most excellent man and a good and faithful preacher, was captured with his regiment at Plymouth, and I found him here.[5] He was quite unwell and confined to his tent. He had a blanket for a bed, and this kept him a little off the ground. There were no boards, beds, or straw. He seemed glad to see me, but I thought him a good deal used up.

Capt. Mackey, of Pennsylvania,[6] asked me to hold service at dusk, and we gathered beneath a large tree just as the sun was sinking beneath the horizon and worshipped God. We sung "America," and I made comments on Psalm xxiii, "The Lord is my Shepherd," etc. In devotion I poured out my soul to God for the President, for Congress, the army and the navy, and for the country, for ourselves and our loved ones at home. It to me was a peculiar service and a solemn hour. When the devotions were over, an hour was spent singing our own national songs. The "Star Spangled Banner," and "The Red, White and Blue," and "Rally Round the Flag, Boys," etc. seemed to have a deeper and holier meaning than ever before. The rebel soldiers gathered just outside the lines, and large numbers of women and negroes. At every place I went, I saw hardly a man that was not a soldier. Gradually, one by one the curious departed, and the gathering gloom was only relieved by the faint shimmering of the stars. We were to learn to do without candles. If sickness or death comes alone and in the dark we must meet it as best we could.

For the present my travels were over, and I sat down, leaning against a tree and looked up into the face of the calm sweet heavens and pondered on the mutations of human life. In my Northern home, my good wife and four dear children that night would bow at the altar, on which the fires of devotion had burned along all the years of our wedded life, and pray for one. They knew not whether he lived in the hands of the enemy or by the chances of battle had been hurried to the solemn walks of the higher life. Those who have been placed in similar circumstances can imagine the drift and sadness of my thoughts. Those who have not, with a sigh of sympathy will lay down this paper and turn to their joys, and their gathering of gold. The hope of the gospel and the love of Jesus were my chief stay, and were indescribably sweet. I probed my soul's motives. I looked squarely into the face of my hope. Was the gospel a vast and immutable truth? Was there a heaven, a God? Are these commotions his work; and through and beyond them is there good for man; is there glory for Jesus? Yes. I saw it all and rejoiced. The stars gilded diadem, a fragment of which I beheld above me, that rests on and adorns the august brow of the Infinite, the Omnipotent, as I closed my eyes seemed but a faint shadow, compared with the magnificence of reality that rose before me, as in faith's inspiration I looked out on that constellation of truths that is revealed in the word of God. Some of the night I thus spent in reverential musings, and then I laid down on the turf of the sweet mother earth and slept.

*Zion's Herald and Wesleyan Journal,* February 15, 1865, p. 25.

# *Letter 12*

Providence, R.I., Dec. 28, 1864

The fair grounds at Macon on three sides are surrounded by an unbroken forest. On the Northern side and towards the town, are the commodious and elegant brick buildings and repair shops. These buildings were constructed by Northern men, and are well done.

On Monday, May 16, we drew our rations, and commenced prison life in camp. Here we drew flour, meal and bacon, and were quite elated. I was kindly invited by Capt. Mackey to mess with him, and as he had plenty of money, and was allowed to send into town by the guards for extras, we got along finely. Chaplain Dixon was better and as we were all fresh captures, we were quite well, and full of hope that we should soon be exchanged. Money was used freely, and we purchased such things as we needed.[1] A gallon of molasses cost twenty-five dollars. A Dutch bake kettle, holding some two gallons, cost thirty-five dollars. When the Plymouth officers first came to Macon, the ladies came and brought small gifts and books, and showed us much sympathy. This class of Union sympathizers soon became known, and were watched and ordered off. I have seen ladies come and walk up and down just beyond the beat of the sentinel, with bundles under their shawls, seeking a chance to slip them in, but being baffled by the viligance of the guards, with downcast and sorrowful face would walk away. These persons were either Union people or had friends in Northern prisons, and gave to us, hoping others would do the same for their friends.

The stockade just in sight was rapidly approaching completion. One day we saw a column of the roughest looking men pass us toward the stockade. They were the captives from the Libby Prison, Richmond, Va. Toward night our company was turned into the stockade with them. A new class of suffering was before me. The men were old prisoners, and pale and haggard. They were ragged, and some partly naked. They were filthy, and covered with vermin.[2] Prison life makes men hard, selfish and rough. Here and there you find a prodigal son or a backslider seeking again the comforts of salvation. The stockade was an enclosure of nearly three acres, surrounded by a strong board fence some sixteen feet high. On the outside, some four feet from the top, a platform, some three feet wide, with a railing, ran entirely round the stockades. On this platform the guards were posted. On the inside, some twelve or fifteen feet from the stockade fence, was a small picket fence. This was the dead line. The guards were instructed to shoot any one who touched the dead line. At the west end of the enclosure was a small brook and the sink. The fence was so built that the stream came in, and for some sixty feet, ran within the enclosure. Some twenty feet of this stream before it entered the sink was used for bathing and washing clothes. As much filth from some manufactories just above found its way into the sink; it was not used for drinking or cooking. Several tubs were set in the slope of ground at the roots of an old tree, and they were filled by a spring in the bank. A well at the other end of the enclosure also furnished us with water. As a thousand men were to be supplied, we found the supply entirely inadequate to the demand. In the brook at all times could be seen a row of men, standing close, one behind the other, bathing themselves and washing their garments. The amount of water was not equal to what would run through a tub two inches in diameter. Of course the clothes could not be very well cleaned. Often no soap could be obtained.

The shelter of the place consisted of two buildings formerly used at the County and State fairs. One was nearly a hundred feet long and some thirty-five feet wide, having a floor. The other was an old stable used for cattle and swine, and very filthy. The one with floor was used for a hospital for the accomodation of the more feeble, and for the field and staff, together with the general officers. There were a few pine and oak trees in the prison that afforded some shelter from the sun. Some three or four hundred found quarters in these buildings, the others couched down wherever they chose to. Many had no shelter from the burning sun, the rain, or the night air. After a while some boards were furnished and some poles and rude roofs could be erected, that helped to keep off the sun and storms. There were no sides, ends or floors, and of course the shelter was but partial. These sheds were for only a part, and large numbers found quarters in the open air.

Our food was much inferior to that given us when in the field outside. We drew several days' rations at a time. Less than a quart of unsifted corn meal, with about two ounces of bacon, a table spoonful of rice, about the same quantity of beans, a spoonful of salt, and sometimes instead of bacon we got two or three spoonfuls of molasses. They pretended to give us soup, but for twenty days at a time I would not get a bit, and when I did it was not a spoonful per day. The rice and beans were issued but a few times. The bacon was often rotten and full of worms. I have seen load after load of meat issued to the officers that looked as filthy as a ham would if thrown into the soft black slush of a pig pen, and drawn out and shaken so it would not drip, and then issued. A quartermaster of mess commissary was appointed by the rebels from among our men, who received the rations and issued them to the squad commissary, who drew for a hundred men. The squads were divided into messes of twenty each. The mess commissary dealt out to each man.[3] Our wood was drawn nearly in the same way. The ration of wood was a small stick each day. This was split with the squad axe, which was issued to us each morning and taken out at night.

The men would use it in turn till each had prepared his wood. It was cut into splinters, and used with the utmost economy. Often our wood would be furnished late, or the axe would not be sent in so that breakfast could not be prepared before noon.

The utensils for cooking were few. For a hundred men eight small skillets, several tin pans, and six or eight tin kettles comprised the total furnished us. The tin was poor, and when burned out we had to go without or do the best we could. A few bricks were furnished us, and we put them together so as to put the skillet on them and build a fire beneath. The corn meal was mixed with water and often without salt, and put in the skillet to bake. The skillets had a cover, and we made a fire above and beneath. By constant practice we learned to get up quite a good loaf, or pone, as the Southerns call them. For some twenty dollars a pound we could obtain soda. By allowing the dough to stand awhile it would become sour, and by adding soda it would sweeten and cause it to rise, and often we would get a loaf of good bread. But having one thing right along it soon became monotonous, and we came to loathe the sight of it. The spoonful of rice would be boiled and make one meal, or the bit of bacon and the rice or beans would be put in a kettle of water and made into soup. By putting in plenty of water we were sure of as much as we could eat, and this was our only full meal. When they gave us five days' rations we would often eat them up in three days, and if we were out of money we must go without. After a while some of the men made ovens of the bricks for baking, and were able to thoroughly cook the meal, which made it more harmless.

As the unsifted meal made coarse and quite indigestible bread, we had to resort to some expedient to sift it. When I entered the Confederacy I had a tin canteen. This we threw into the fire and melted the halves apart, and took one for a plate and the other we punched full of holes with a sharp bit of iron, and made of it quite a respectable sieve. At one time this was the only sieve in prison so far as I knew, and it was set at work early and kept well at it till dark. Presently a lady in Macon sent in a piece of wire cloth some fifteen inches square, which was fitted with a frame and did the work much better. Each man must do his own cooking. Some took hold quite handy, and others seemed to view the operation with some modest measure of disgust. Often four or five would club together and take turns in cooking. When a new captive would arrive we would invite him to dine. The first day would pass pretty well. The second he would begin to look around, make inquiries, and look over his rations. The third day the starch would be pretty well taken out, and off would come the coat, and you would see him experimenting with his Indian dough. To some men it seemed almost like breaking the bones to bend them, but they had to come down. Some had not much genius for cooking, and would do it poorly, and soon became sick. No servants were allowed. We thought our treatment as bad as could be, but the privates must have suffered more than we did. As the time for which I entered the service has expired, and I am mustered out, I will drop my official signature.[4]

*Zion's Herald and Wesleyan Journal,* March 1, 1865, p. 33.

Providence, R.I., Feb. 20, 1865

Every grade of rank, from lieutenant to general, was treated with the same cold, haughty indignity. The Confederate authorities wished the ranking officer to assume command in the prison. Brig. Gen. Wessels being the ranking officer, assumed command and appointed an assistant adjutant.[1] The officers were divided into squads of one hundred, and placed under the command of the ranking officer of the squad, who also had his adjutant. The commanders of squads were expected to report to the commandant of the prison, and he was to report to the rebel authorities. So far as it was an advantage to us the officers would report, but we did not feel as though it was our work to govern and keep order, and so save them work. Then a commissary for the prison was appointed from our officers to receive and issue the rations. Each squad had its commissary. Each squad was further divided into messes of twenty, with its commissary. This organization I think originated with our officers, and secured a fair and just distribution of all the food the rebels allowed us to have. Our rations consisted of a cup of corn meal per day to each man. Several days' rations were issued at a time. A small piece of bacon would be issued for five days that a man would eat at a single meal. Sometimes we would get a table spoonful of rice per day, and oftener none at all. A few times we drew a handful of wormy beans. Sometimes they gave us molasses instead of meat.

They pretended to give us soft soap, but I did not get a spoonful once a week. Keeping clean with what they furnished was of course out of the question. At first they gave us a few drops of vinegar to each man. The vinegar was made by putting corn meal in vats and filling them with water, and the sun would soon sour the water, when it would be drawn off and served out to us, but this lasted only a few days, and was abandoned. The vinegar was white, and full of meal, bran, and bits of cob. Each man did his own washing and cooking. Wood in small quantities was furnished, which we split with axes furnished us at the rate of one for each hundred prisoners. A shovel for each squad was allowed. At first the miners attempted to appropriate an axe or shovel. No one then could have an axe or shovel to use till the one missing was returned. Of course this brought us to terms. We had to be our own scavengers, and clean up the ground and remove the filth from the sink. Carts were sent in with negro drivers, and for a time we obeyed and threw the garbage heaps into the carts; but after a little we would not do it, and soldiers or negroes were sent to do it.

Bricks were furnished, and we set them up one upon another, and so made a rude range for cooking. We had one well only for a long time. Afterwards two more were dug. Even these were inefficient to supply us with water, and the small brook that came across our corner of the prison pen ran some ten or fifteen feet inside the dead line before it entered the sink. The water was freely used, although we well knew it ran past several places where it received contributions that would not particularly recommend it to the fastidious. Some old tubs were set beside the brook, and fed by a small spring. Here we were to bathe, and those who had shirts used to wash them. Our sink was composed of planks resting on some scantlings thrown across the ditch through which the brook ran, and as there was no seat many a poor weak fellow would fall. The dead line was near, and if a man staggered he was in danger of being shot. The whole place was excessively filthy, and soon became alive with vermin. No one could escape. Skirmishing through our garments seam by seam, and stich by stich, after the impertinent intruders, was a daily and almost hourly necessity. At first this was extremely disgusting, and I used to seek to keep out of sight, but all shame at last went. Officers of all ranks almost naked could be seen on every hand, earnestly engaged in the pursuit of the foe. How often have I spent an hour in skirmishing my garments, and then in fancied triumph sat down to read or converse, when a sharp nip at the back of my heel would remind me that perseverence and eternal vigilance is required to exterminate the graybacks.

I remember on one occasion a "fresh fish" in the shape of a fine officer, whose rank shall be nameless, was most reluctantly introduced to our society, and because of his rank was requested to take charge of a certain section of the prison. His fair flesh had not been laced by the tiny teeth of the graybacks, and when he saw men half nude all about him making things snap, his high-bred soul revolted, and he ordered that no more depredations on the little ones should be perpetrated in his department. You have heard how once upon a time a certain monarch found unwelcome visitors coming up upon his coach. I think I have heard or read sometime or somewhere that history repeats itself. It was a long time before he would break his own rule. Many of my good readers may be utterly unable to appreciate the task upon his patience created by what was going on under his vest, but I think your humble servant has an experience that enables him most feelingly to sympathize with the assaulted and unfortunate gentleman.

We attempted to obtain boxes from the North, but could receive none. The prisoners of the "Hotel de Libby," at Richmond, found themselves vastly worse off, so far as help from home was concerned, at Macon than at Richmond. When there they received a few of the many boxes sent them, and what they did get was all clear gain. Flour, butter, sugar, corn, starch, rice, hams, drief beef, canned fruits and meats, dried fruits, clothing, stationery, etc., in small quantities did reach them. Of course they stole nine tenths, but then one tenth was an inestimable boost to men that by it were kept from starvation. But here not a thing could reach us. Even the letters sent by our friends, a few of which were given us, had the half of the sheet not written on torn off. A box was prepared for the reception of letters, and we were informed that we might write to our friends. Many at once joyfully prepared letters for home. We were ordered to write plainly, on one side of a half sheet, and interlined, and concerning personal and family affairs only. The letters were to be left open for examination. Of course we understood that only those who spoke well of our treatment and our prison keepers, could hope to have his letter go through. All wrote most encouraging and cheerful letters. But even then they did not send them as they agreed to do, but kept them in the prison office for weeks and months till large bundles accumulated.[2]

We were eager to obtain news from home, and of the army. Letters came to here and there one. The chaplain was not in good favor with those pioneers of progress for reasons that will presently appear, and of course got no letters.

Newspapers were not generally allowed. Sometimes when there was no news, or when there was an account of a "Union defeat," or when some mean low slang appeared, they would allow some to come in the prison. We used to watch the trains of cars as they passed near us, and could read in the loads of wounded and the movement of troops something of what was going on. The lies told in the papers were so transparent, that through them we could read of the steady and glorious advance of our arms. When our army seemed checked, a gloom like the pall of night would fall on us; and when the foe was defeated and routed, the golden glory of an elevated and almost heavenly joy would gush from every soul.

*Zion's Herald and Wesleyan Journal,* March 22, 1865, p. 45.

# ☙ *Letter 14*

A chaplain in a rebel prison is in one of the most uncongenial positions. He is not *wanted* there. The fixings are not *precisely* adjusted to his taste. But I would preach. I would pray to my God. Chaplain Dixon, of whom I have spoken before, a Christian gentleman, stood squarely and grandly up to his work. We held several communions together, and strengthened each other's hands. In all our public services we shared in the duties.

I had not been more than a day or two in the stockade at Macon before Major Bates,[1] a fine and noble Christian officer, spoke to me about holding service, and we arranged for an evening sermon that week. I did intend to preach, but not feeling well, Chaplain Dixon changed work with me and preached the sermon, while I conducted the opening service. Our meeting was held at the end of an old building erected for a store and show room at the fairs held on the grounds. One of the shutters resting on the steps and an old bench made our pulpit. Several had soldiers' hymn books, and the singing was good. I read a chapter and offered prayer. In my devotions I asked God to "bless the President of these United States, his cabinet, the Congress, the army and navy." I asked God to "give wisdom to our officers, and confuse the counsels of our foes; and so give victory to the loyal armies of the nation," etc. After singing again, Chaplain Dixon preached a good and appropriate sermon, and we retired to rest. The Libby prisoners just sent down from Richmond had not heard a sermon from their own chaplains in a long time, and seemed much edified. Several times in the day or two before the Sabbath it came to me indirectly that the rebels would not allow us to pray for the president and the army as I had done. Sabbath evening Chaplain Dixon conducted the introductory service and I preached the sermon. In his own style, but squarely and directly, did he come to the subject and pray for the president and the country. The audience was large, intelligent and attentive, but nothing occurred of special importance. The allusions in the sermon were loyal, but not such as need exasperate anyone.

The next day I think it was, one of the general officers in the prison said to me as he was passing, "Chaplain, the rebel authorities did not like your sermon the other night." I replied, "General, it was not me that preached, it was Chaplain Dixon." "Well, your prayer then," said he, "it was you who gave the offense, by praying for the President and the United States." "But, General," I said, "cannot we pray here among our own officers just as we pray in our regiments in the service?" "Of course," said he, "it does not offend me, but I thought I would mention that it gave them great offense," and he passed along. It was soon rumored about the prison that the rebels were not going to allow the chaplains to pray for the president. The indignation was intense. There were gentlemen there that were not particularly interested in the chaplains or chaplain's work, but they were patriotic and heroes, and proudly and thoroughly hated rebels and the rebellion. When they heard of our position they called on us and paid us special attention, and cheered us with sound and hearty words. But they went further than words of cheer, and treated us to the most generous hospitality that the place and circumstances afforded. Do not laugh while I tell you what fare they had to offer. When captured I came down on a canteen and kept it close, and had it when turned into the stockade. Our meal was not sifted, and contained bits of coarse bran, cob and kernels of corn. Melting apart the oval halves of the canteen, of one we made a plate and of the other a sieve by punching holes in it with a bit of sharp iron. With this we sifted the meal. The ingenuity of the others by different methods arrived at the same result. This bran and bits of cob was taken, and in a skillet burned so as to make a substitute for coffee. With this I was treated. It was an attention to be grateful for, and I trust that I appreciated it, but the indulgence was almost too much for me. When one has been on short allowance and then is suddenly introduced to high living, you know that care must be taken or injurious and often fatal consequences may follow. The battle between my appetite and my judgment was hot and fierce as I closed my lips on the nectar that a generous hospitality proffered me.

Some of those men were rough and stern, especially those of Streight's raiders who had been a long time in the prison, and were kept back from exchange.[2] Some of them allowed that they were not much devoted to religious things. One of them said that he had not been to church for sixteen years, but burning with indignation toward the rebels for interfering with us praying as we chose, with more patriotism than piety, said, "he would be damned if the chaplain shouldn't pray for the President."

Almost every officer attended service, and all entered with amazing enthusiasm into the devotions. The singing was like the loud, grand swell of song at camp meeting. The deep and enthusiastic responses to the patriotic sentiments contained in the prayers came from lips unaccustomed to saying amen. Thus in a feverish expectation things went on a few days, till one evening when it devolved on me to preach and on Bro. Dixon to offer the opening prayer. All were gathered close about as I stepped on the platform and read the first hymn. As I closed and turned about to hand the hymn book to Bro. Dixon, Captain Tabb, Commandant of the prison,[3] stepped upon the platform and said, saluting me, "Chaplain, I have come to say to you that we cannot allow you to pray for the President of the United States and the success of your army and defeat of ours, as you have done." Chaplain Dixon arose and stepped upon the platform just by his side, and among the audience was the most perfect silence. The guards were within hearing with muskets at the soldiers, stopped walking their beats on the top of the stockade and listened. The gunners stood to their post beside the twelve-pound bass Napoleon that was trained upon the place where we stood. Three or four aged citizens stood in a group by themselves a little to the left by a tree near the dead line. This was a new, and I felt quite delicate, position.

I thought it best to take the Captain only on a single point and replied, "Captain, do I understand you to command me as Chaplain in the United States Army, acting in my official capacity among our own officers, not to pray for the President of the United States?" "Yes," said he, "I command you not to do it." I knew altogether too much about military affairs to attempt to directly disobey an order, and saw that to gain my point I must give a semblance of obedience, and then draw him into an argument, in which I hoped to confuse, and then, rout him, and so gain my purpose.

"Very well," said I, "you give me a written order to that effect and I will obey it. But, Captain, are you aware what kind of an order this is that you are giving me? It strikes me as very strange indeed. Your chaplains in our prisons pray loud and long for Jeff. Davis and the Confederate States, and no one cares a thing for it, and now you come and attempt to interfere with our consciences and our prayers before God." "But your government does interfere, I think, with our chaplains, and prevent their praying for the Confederacy." "No," I said, "you are mistaken; they never interfere with the devotions of the prisoners of war. That is worse than the Roman Inquisition."

"If we were out in the city and interfered with your people it would be different, but what little comfort we can get from our devotion it is not right or manly to deprive us of. If we were doing anything that unfitted the prisoners for your control it would be different; but a long as we do not interfere with your prison discipline we have a right to preach, pray, lecture on temperance, spiritualism, God, or no God, play ball, pitch quoit, wrestle or any other thing that may amuse or interest us." He replied that "it offended the citizens." "O," said I, "I thought this was a *military prison,* and I did not know before that a military institution was under *civil* control." "But," he replied, "the soldiers hear it," pointing to the stockade along which the guards were posted. "Well," said I, "that is nothing to us, we did not put them there." He laughed, and replied that if our government allowed their chaplains to pray as they pleased he would permit us to do the same. By this time, as you may imagine, I had become decidedly interested in my subject, and placing my hand familiarly on his shoulder was proceeding to introduce sundry other reasons why he should mind his own business, and leave us alone, when he said, "I permit you, I permit you," repeating it with kind and feeling earnestness. I thanked him and saluting each other we parted, he retiring into the building, and I turned and again announced the hymn, which was sung with a will. Chaplain Dixon offered the first prayer, and when he called on God to lead our father Abraham with the nation in triumph for its troubles we all said amen.

*Zion's Herald and Wesleyan Journal,* April 12, 1865, p. 57.

Providence, R.I. [ca. March 21, 1865]

When Captain Tabb had gone, and we were left to conduct our devotion as we pleased, we used our liberty to a purpose. I believe much good was done. Not long after the adventure related in my previous letter, one of the officers died and I was called upon to conduct the funeral services. In the opening of the service I said: "My brethren, we are convened to pay the last tribute of respect to a hero, who has fallen a martyr to a cause as sacred as the death of Jesus," and proceeded to make such remarks as I deemed appropriate to the wants of the noble men about me. Just as I finished the above sentence, I cast my eye up, and just to the left, surrounded by a few citizens, stood Capt. Tabb. Like a flash I could see that the party was agitated, and that Tabb was mad.

Sometimes since I have thought that perhaps it was a little rash to curse the Confederacy to hell and ask God to help and expedite the thing, but it did not occur to me to be so then. To be sure I saw danger, and the blood of murdered men, but that made no impression upon us. How the martyrs and heroes of the olden time could stand it to suffer and endure as they did, for a long time was a mystery, and I am not at all sure that I know now, yet it does not seem so much a mystery as it did. As I looked into the muzzle of that cannon trained on my head, and knew the instant death that a single jerk of the lanyard would bring it did not more intimidate me than did the chirp of the cricket that sung by the dead line. The remark was strong, and strictly speaking I should wish to modify it somewhat before defending it. The *Christian Index,* the Baptist paper printed in Macon, did me the honor to notice me, and with its ecclesiastical lash, gave me a good sound thrashing for my impiety, ignorance, infidelity, and "abolition hellishness," as in their charming and detectable Christian refinement they loved to call us and our principles. Now there are some charming sentences in that column that I was the occasion of calling forth, and if it were not that these letters are not running on through so many number, I would quote some of them.[1]

Our prayer meetings were held beneath the open sky and at dusk, and before they closed it would be dark, save the fitful glare of the fires that burned along the dead line to enable the sentinels to fire well. In the audience were good men whom abuse had soured, and their prayers were bold and terrible denunciations that almost chilled my own blood, and I do not wonder that they stirred up the rebels. But if we knew we would not tell who cursed what God is cursing. At such times the rebel officers would grow insolent, and one day a certain man who had not the fear of Jeff. before his eyes, told the officer that he had best beware how he exasperated those officers, for there were some desperate men among them, and if enraged, some man's life might possibly be in danger. "What suppose you the fifty men with muskets could do, that you bring in as a guard, if these twelve or fifteen hundred officers should attempt to seize them?" After that the commandant seemed more careful.

Attempts to escape employed the attention of a large number, and the hope of success kept many a poor fellow from sinking in despair.[2] The method adopted first was to tunnel. This was done by sinking a hole large enough for a man to go down, about three feet, and then run a lead to the ground beyond the stockade fence, where they were to break out and run. It was hoped that a large number would be enabled to get out in a night, and that many would get off. We never succeeded in completing one. The rebels had a spy in the prison, or else some one would "blow" on us, and defeat the plan. Every morning, and often at night, we had a roll call. About fifty boys and old men would be brought in and posted across the pen not far from the centre, and the officers were all driven to one end, and then counted through one by one as men count sheep they sell. Often the count would not come out right, and then we had to be counted again.

At roll call an officer and several guards would go through the grounds, with ramrods taken from their muskets, and run them into the ground in any place to see if they could find a "gopher hole," as they called them. The men who dug the holes, the "Johnnies," were called "gophers."

One night the working party was discovered at work, and Captain Tabb came in with a guard and ordered the officers to fill it up. Those standing by worked awhile, when Tabb turned to one of our officers lying near by, and commanded him to get up and help fill it up. Tabb said he should help; the major said he would not. Tabb then commanded one of the guards to shoot him, but the guard hesitated to fire, when Tabb seized the musket and began to beat the officer with it. The major did not yield, and presently Tabb desisted.

One day an officer was late in getting down to the place of roll call, and Tabb had him marched out of prison and made him stand for a long time in front of the hospital near the prison gate. He had not eaten breakfast, and none was given him. About noon some of the officers in the hospital gave the one standing in the sun some of their scanty fare. One of our officers, detailed in the hospital to help take care of our own sick, feared the rebels would blame him for allowing the convalescent officers to give this man food, and so he went out, and as they told me, took it from him. The rebel soldiers standing by were so enraged at this inhumanity, that they took some of their own rations and gave the man a dinner. There were several complaints that some of our own officers who got power did not use it so as to do the greatest good to their brethren. These were exceptions, however, for as a general thing all stood noble by one another.

One night, just as dusk was coming on, I heard the report of a musket down in the direction of the brook in the west end of the stockade at Macon. Like a flash it was told through the camp that another officer was shot. I ran out to see, and Lieut. O. Gerson, of New York was lying amid some men who gathered about him.[3] The ball passed in at the right shoulder just over the shoulder-blade, down through into his vitals, and about midnight he died. He conversed some time, and then fell asleep. He must have been standing with his back partly toward the guard. I went down and examined the place next morning, and the pool of blood on the ground were he fell showed that he was from ten to fifteen feet from the dead line, with face from it, when the guard shot him. I went to the hospital just outside, and held service at his burial.

I wished to know for myself how this would come out, and so kept my eye upon the matter. After a day or two the boy, whose name was

Belger, and who was about fifteen years of age, disappeared. About a month afterward I said to one of the subordinate officers, "What did they do with young Belger that shot Gerson?"[4] At first he did not seem to wish to tell me, but as we were on good terms, and as I urged him, he told me they made him a sergeant, and gave him a furlough for twenty days. The guards were encouraged to shoot us. There was no sorrow when we were shot at or when we died. The impression among us was that they were glad we were out of the way.

Fourth of July was a great day. All were full of hope, and wished to make some manifestation, but no one seemed to know exactly what it was best to do. When roll call was over, about nine o'clock, and just as the count was being closed, one of the officers was seen with a small American flag erected, and with a defiant step he marched up and down before the line of guards posted across the enclosure. Our officers commenced to cheer, and as he marched back and forth, cheer after cheer went up for the dear old flag. The officer of the guard seemed confused, and acted as though he feared some attempt to spring a plot. Quietly and rapidly he drew his men together, and without saying a word to any of our men, marched them out. The guards were at once increased along the stockade platform, the four cannon trained on the inside of the prison were manned, and everything prepared for a demonstration. All was commotion outside, and all was excitement within the prison. I was in the hospital at the time, and could not get into the prison pen, for communication between hospital and prison had been cut off for two or three days. But I could hear the commotion and the comments of the guards, and climbing up into a window I could see and hear. The crowd, on the retirement of the guards, went into an old building within the stockade, and organized a meeting. Chaplain Dixon opened it with prayer, and as was usual with him, with his warm and holy petitions for the President and the country, fired the audience for the services to follow. National songs were sung, speeches were made, toasts were offered. The excitement increased; louder and grander was the storm of passionate enthusiasm swelling out in song and speech. The rebel soldiers caught it and seemed moved. The eyes of the sick and dying began to snap, and all their faces blushed with laughter and hope. The rebel officers, fully armed and in full uniform, moved rapidly from point to point. The meeting had been in full blast for about two hours, when a colonel whose name now has escaped me, was called out. His was the most radical, bold and noble speech. At this stage an order was sent into the prison to break up the meeting and disperse. They had enjoyed the good time and had been refreshed, and soon all retired slowly to their quarters beneath the huts and trees. The only penalty inflicted was taking the command of the camp out of the hands of the colonel. His name went up with us as it went down among the rebels.[5]

Perhaps it was a cruel joy we felt when the large trains of wounded daily came down from the front above Atlanta, when Sherman with his legions were smashing the rebellion. 'Twas not the suffering that gave us joy, but when the trains were large, and the depot was full of the maimed and dying, we knew that the infernal power of Jeff. was being broken, and we were glad.

*Zion's Herald and Wesleyan Journal,* May 10, 1865, p. 73.

# *Letter 16*

Wheeling, West Va., April 24, 1865

The officers that died at Macon were buried in the woods about a quarter of a mile back from the prison camp. They were put in plain coffins, and with their garments on, buried respectably. A detail of our own officers connected with the hospital as nurses or attendants usually went and buried the dead. We did not wish the rebels to touch the sacred forms of our martyred dead. The true and constant friend of the prisoners was the negro. When the battle-storm was sweeping the Confederacy down and the tide was beating its barriers in, the authorities shut out our papers, and it was difficult to get news. When Sherman was approaching, we became so eager to hear that a man offered a watch worth two hundred dollars for a newspaper, and could not get it. At that time I have seen a negro come in among us and look stealthily about to see if he was observed, and then quickly take a paper from his bosom and hand it to some officer, and instantly disappear without even speaking. I desired at this time to know how things were going up in town. At this time I was paroled to go out to the hospital and see the sick and help bury the dead. So I put myself in communication with a negro belonging to one of the "fustest" families in Macon, and through him got at the private political table talk. One day he had a great piece of news for me. Sherman had "whip Johnson and *smash* him all to pieces, and when Massa tell Missus she jes faint rite dead away."

None but the true secesh negroes were ever permitted to come near the Union prisoners. Among those they could best trust, I never found one false; I have heard of some, but never met one. One day a negro came into the stockade with a load of rations. He had on his wagon a large box, perhaps three feet square. After unloading, several of the officers were standing about, when one proposed to put Lieut. Willson into the box.[1] It was done, and he was covered with meal sacks, and Sambo with a grave and solemn pace drove out past the guard, and down to the barn-yard where he kept his beast. He got down and took out his mules and left his wagon standing in the yard and went away home. When night came, the officer started for the front, but after a day or two he was brought back. The rebel authorities tried hard to find out how he escaped, but no one would tell them. Some days several, in one way or another, would get out, and a humorous fellow among us, when the officer asked how they escaped, said that one of the officers had a spring board, and used to jump them out over the top of the fence.

One day a young officer from Massachusetts attempted to escape off as one of the guards, and going out as others were going in; he obtained a pair of dirty grey pants, made, I think, of an old meal sack, that somehow was "obtained"; he got an old slouch hat and a coarse cotton shirt; he passed the guard and got out of prison, and was going along when a rebel called out to him to stop, and on coming up said, "You can't come that game on me, for your shirt is too clean. I know you are not a rebel." Poor fellow! He came back quite reluctantly. A dirty shirt would have passed him out.

As the summer advanced, the news of the advance of Sherman and the proximity of the raiding parties filled us with hopes of deliverance. One day near the close of July, an order was posted for six hundred of the officers to get ready to leave.[2] The camp was full of joy. The rebels gave us to understand that it was for exchange. All were eager to go. With my good wishes they left us. What became of them for some time was not known to us. Captain Aigan and Lieutenant Durfee left with the others, and I was left alone. Two days after another six hundred prisoners arrived. Another hour passed as we were being counted out and rolls prepared. They marched us to the cars and took us off for the night. I suppose they did not wish the citizens of Macon to see such a crowd as we were. The train consisted of box cars full of filth and vermin. We reached Gordon, a station on the Central Georgia Railroad at the junction of the road from Milledgeville, about eight o'clock in the morning. The day was charming; the railway accommodations here were quite extensive and well arranged, and several trains met here. There were several good buildings, and in one was a "Wayside Home," a kind of free hospital and retreat for soldiers. Just as our train came up, about a dozen ladies came sailing out from the wayside home and moved down toward the train. We had not seen many ladies in the South. These were neatly attired, in light dresses, and with flowers in their hair they presented a most charming appearance, as with a plate in each hand, on which was a cup of coffee, a sandwich, some cold meat and bread, and a piece of cake, they came gaily sailing down toward us. I was in the front car. The guards with muskets sat in the doors of the cars, three in each door, and we were crowded in behind them.

Just as the group of ladies came close to the first car, one of the guards said, "these are Yanks." The first lady and leading spirit of the group halted as sudden as though she had been shot, and turning up that pretty nose of hers, said in that tone and style so natural to the daughters of the sunny South, "O! I thought they were some of our people," and turning upon her heel marched off with that air of ineffable disdain that some of my readers can better imagine than my pen describe. In a few moments we were hurried away. Some said in thirty minutes and others three hours after Gen. Stoneman with his cavalry, who was after us, struck the road at this point. At least it was shortly after, and finding how near he came to obtaining us, I presume his good nature was not particularly improved, and after the most approved method he proceeded to mix things somewhat. As track and train and building went up in smoke, or were "fixed," in my mind's eye, I see those fair damsels with raven locks and flashing eye, taking a bee line for the wilderness. Perhaps it is a little naughty in me, but I have often thought that I would have called it square with her if I could have stood about a hundred rods from those smoking ruins, and as they swept past me have said, "Ladies, have you seen anything of *our people*' around here?"

Wherever the train stopped the negroes brought us watermelons, for which we gave them Confederate money. They seemed such a luxury. About five o'clock in the afternoon of July 29 the train reached Savannah, Ga. The train stopped in the street and we were ordered out of the cars and formed in line. This took some time. Multitudes gathered about us of both sexes and all shades. Just at my right in a large elegant brick mansion, a lady threw up the window and shook out that detestable emblem of all meanness, a rebel flag. What could I do? The paving stones were all fast. I had no brick, and the only defense left was to show our contempt for her and it by spitting at it.

We were marched into a stockade, built on the brick wall or fence surrounding the yard of the Marine hospital. It rained that night. Obtaining a board, I propped it up and slept well on it, being above the running water. The majority were less fortunate, and slept or laid in the slush and mud. Chaplain Dixon came with me, and we remained here about one month. The food was better and more abundant than at any place I was at. The hospital building was shut out from us by the stockade and dead line built across that end of the yard. The sick for a long time could obtain no attention or medicine. At last a small tent was pitched in the yard for them, but not a thing put in it for comfort, not a straw. The surgeons of our army that were held acted nobly, and did all that could be done, but having no remedies they could give but partial aid. After a time, small tents were issued to the prisoners, which helped to keep off the rain and sun. Sometime after our arrival the hospital building was opened to our sick. I attempted to get permission to go to the hospital to visit the sick. Lieut. Col. Wayne, the commandant of the prison, was a coarse, rough man, and it was said he came from Connecticut, and being a copperhead, entered the Southern army.[3] One day I sent out a note asking permission to visit a sick friend. After a long time it was returned approved, and I went out. In the mean time one of our officers had died, and I asked permission to attend his funeral. The response was that they could furnish their own chaplains. While I was out, however, the lady having charge, and by the way she was good and kind to our men, said to me that she had sent for her minister to attend the funeral, but did not know that he would come. Some eight or ten of our officers were there, and I proposed to read the lessons and attend to the usual service. I felt we enjoyed it much. After the service I stepped in to speak personally to the others, when the Colonel came along and roughly asked on how he did. The officer made no reply. I then asked the Colonel if he would allow me to come in each day and vist the sick. He said, "no." "This is not Macon," said he, and "you are under different orders here." I attempted to plead the case when he roughly cut me off. At this the officer of the day stepped

up and said I had better return to the prison, and so I was forced away
to the prison without so much as being allowed to speak to the rest of
the sick, although I was in the room with them.

*Zion's Herald and Wesleyan Journal,* May 24, 1865, p. 81.

# &* *Letter 17*

Wheeling, West Va., May 10, 1865

I spent nearly a month in the stockade at Savannah. From time to time we held service. Sometimes we had preaching, and sometimes social meetings. In every place I tried to obtain a Bible; I could get none. I wrote letters to the Methodist preachers wherever I was, inviting them to call, or at least, send me a Bible. No one ever called, and I got no Bible. At one time, in answer to my request, I received a few papers and tracts published by the Church South. They were bitter and hard on the North. Many of the most earnest and bitter were Southern Methodists. From a fact or two, perhaps it will appear that Methodists in the North were as beastly on the other side, though I hope not so unchristian. At one time, at Macon, there were ten ministers, three chaplains and seven officers, and every one I understood belonged to the Methodist Church. Chaplain Dixon was cap-tured with a chaplain that belonged to *the church.* The *regular man* at once went to the rebels and told them he had not made up his mind which side was right and that if he got out, he would not enter the service again. He went home in a few weeks. Chaplain Dixon stood aloof. He made no apology for being there, but went to helping the wounded and to comforting the dying. Him they kept more than five months, and treated him like a dog.

The rebels put up a small building for a kind of sutler's shop, and to put rations in, as they were brought into the stockade. The work was done by negro carpenters. I used to amuse myself by watching them at their work. I did not see but they used tools as handy, and planned work as well as any one would. The conversation among themselves was as dignified and intelligent as you would be apt to hear from a gang of working men in the North. To be sure, they were city negroes, and better bred than those could be on the plantations. One day I wanted some nails to fix up my bed. I went out where the negroes were at work. Some rebel soldiers were guarding them, and a white man also had charge of the gang. I carelessly walked up behind a fine looking young negro, and said in a low voice, "Give me some nails." He did not seem to move a muscle, or turn his head to look around. He stood a moment, and then went a few steps and picked up a hammer lying on the ground. He then went to the nail keg and took up a handful of nails, and spent a moment in laying them straight in his hand. He then walked off to the opposite side of the building from where I stood, and facing about, took a leisurely survey of the state of affairs. His hands were crossed behind him. After a little, he came round where I stood, coming close, and turned his back toward me. I put out my hand and touched his knuckles below, when he opened his hand, and the nails fell into mine. In a moment he walked off to his work. In the whole transaction he did not speak, did not seem in the least to notice me. Perhaps some one will be interested to know that a keg of nails cost six hundred dollars.

The sink for the prison was a trench dug across one end of the yard; but becoming so loathsome, other arrangements were eventually made. The slaves were sent to fill the old trench. The most of the number were women and girls. The overseer seemed to have no shame about sending women to perform such a task. Most of the slaves were partly white. Their arms were naked and their lower limbs were partly exposed. They seemed to be healthy and happy. They watched us with a great deal of seeming interest.

One afternoon it was announced in prison that the chaplains and surgeons would go next morning to be exchanged. We were much elated. In the evening Chaplain Dixon preached a fine sermon; and at the close, I made some remarks. It seemed a time of deep interest, and at its close I said: "We go out from among you, and the only pain we feel is that you are to be left behind; but one thing we can do—we can pray for you. Now we may not meet again on the earth, but so many of you as will promise to try and meet us in heaven, please raise your right hands." By the faint light of the moon that came, breaking through the clouds in the west, and the glare that came from the fires on the dead line, some ten steps off, I could see that every hand went up. The service closed, and for half an hour those dear men gathered about us, shaking hands and with tears bidding us God speed. When the crowd was broken, and most were gone, there came to me a fine young lieutenant, who had lost his right arm. I knew him well. Frail and young and fair, some mother mourned his absence. Too gentle for that rough life! As he came, I saw the big tears standing in his soft eye. "Chaplain," said he, "I haven't a right hand any more, but I raised up my left hand and the piece of this arm that is left on my shoulder, and won't that do as well?" "God sees my heart," he repeated, "and I want you to pray for me." We mingled our tears, and parted. I trust we shall meet again.

The next morning at half past three we were all ready to go. No call was made for us. The day went by and the order was repeated, and next morning we were sent from Savannah. Before leaving, we took many names to write to friends a word of cheer. Our party consisted of nine, two chaplains and seven surgeons. We expected to meet a party from Charleston, and with them go through the lines to Hilton Head. On we went to Charleston, and hope began to droop. In the car was a confederate soldier, a kind looking old man, sitting just behind me. At one time I looked around, and he was eating his lunch. He had a roasted sweet potato. He gave me a piece, and also a bit of bread and meat. It would be useless to attempt to tell how that potato tasted. It was not much the lack of quantity, as it was the *kind* of food.

Not far from noon, we entered Charleston. The cars stopped out of town, and we were marched in. A few negroes sat with a few vegetables to sell by the sides of the streets. The negroes looked kindly upon us. The Irish and German women seemed to pity us. The Southern women made us feel like throwing brickbats. The stores were mostly closed. The grass was rank, and a few cows were feeding. Here and there we saw a pig. As we were waiting at the office of the provost marshal, I gave a boy a dollar to get the party some apples, as he said they had some at the store a little distance off. He brought me three little knotty, tasteless things. It was the best he could do.

We were sent to a house on Broad Street used for the non-combatants' prison. We passed the Work House and Roper Hospital, Marine Hospital, and Jail in which the officers were confined under fire. Just as we were passing, a fine shell exploded in the air, just above our heads. We were put in a building perhaps one hundred rods off from the Roper Hospital. We had plenty of room and a chance to bathe in a bath house near our quarters. Here we got flour and fresh beef. Obtaining money, we secured some sweet potatoes and tomatoes. We purchased some rice. The ever present and ever kind negro again helped us, and we lived with some little comfort.

The city looked like a ruin. No men were to be seen, save here and there an old man. Negroes were passing to and fro to their work on the fortifications. Soldiers in small numbers could be seen, and a few officers were gallanting with the ladies. They used to come and gaze, as children go to Barnum's.

Perhaps the deep interest connected with our stay at Charleston arose from our being placed under fire.[1] This barbarism of placing the Union officers who were prisoners of war under fire, I will explain. For many months the United States force stationed on Morris Island in Charleston Harbor, had been throwing shells into the city. The enemy had been constantly enraged at this, and sought to compel our government to suspend the bombardment. The method was this:

On Friday, June 10, great commotion of joy was caused at Macon, Ga., by an order for fifty ranking officers. Five generals, eleven colonels, twenty-five lieutenant colonels and nine majors left, supposing they were to be exchanged. We bid them go in peace, and gave them the names of our wives and mothers that they might drop them a line to know of our state. Judge of our rage when we learned that they were placed in the shell district at Charleston. The object was to compel our men not to shell the city. When our government was about to put a like number of their officers under fire, the rebels said, "Let us exchange them," and they did so.

On Wednesday, July 27, another order came, and six hundred went. They tried to make us think it was for exchange, but we could not trust them. They went under fire. In a few days three or four hundred more were brought into the city, and early in September the six hundred at Savannah were added, making not far from sixteen hundred in all. The four buildings to which I referred stand on four sides of a square; and if shells came into the city, they would stand a chance to strike here. Our forces soon learned the location, and aimed to not hit the buildings; but Charleston is not a large town, and the wind, or an unequal charge of powder, or a random aim in the night would send the shells in rather close proximity. The shells came all about us. We spent much time in watching the shells and their effect. After a while we got perfectly cool and could study the matter as quietly as a child would look at the stars.

But God would not have us harmed. I have seen hundreds of shells by night and by day thrown near us and explode just by or above us. One passed so near as to set a man whirling. Another tore the sleeve of an officer's coat. One passed down through the building and struck a table around which several were just going to eat some corn bread, and spoiled the ration. A man was taking his comfort on a bench, when a shell struck one end of it, and sent him sprawling. But from first to last not a drop of blood was drawn on a Union officer. They hit *other people.* One night I most distinctly remember: I had an old bunk, and taking a door from its hinges, I made a bed by laying the door as to sleep on it. That night the Swamp Angel seemed to have the range on the burnt district, just between the ruins of the Catholic Church and our quarters.[2]

For a while I watched them with a dull, declining interest. Like a star they shone distinctly, and seemed for two or three miles, as though they would come directly into my eyes, and then by the range I would see that they would go aside or fall short. I slept as sweetly that night as in any night of my life. The music lulled me to repose.

Sometime in September about six hundred rebel officers were put under fire on Morris Island.[3] The enemy asked Gen. Foster to exchange them, but he would not. A few days before I left Charleston, the yellow fever broke out, and some cases were reported on the next street to our prison, and shortly after I was released, all the officers were removed to Columbia, S.C. No private soldiers were put under fire. When we all shall be sleeping, the last sleep, history will say the right word about this vast barbarism of placing unarmed and innocent men up to be shot at.

*Zion's Herald and Wesleyan Journal,* May 31, 1865, p. 85.

# *Letter 18*

Wheeling, West Va., May 1865

The deep and thrilling joy that inspired us as we were ordered to fall in on the morning of the twenty-third of September can hardly be appreciated by one that has not for months been a prisoner in the hands of such scamps as Jeff. Davis and Company.[1] Farewell ye night vigils in which we inspected the curious movements and effects of the shells, in which we sought to interpret the signals from the steeple of St. Michael's or curiously watched the blockade runners as their low, white elegant forms went or came from the sea.

Captain Aigan and Lieutenant Durfee were in the city. When I left Savannah I gave my woolen undershift and stockings to a minister who was an officer and unwell. At Charleston a member of the legislature obtained my vest and the tops of my boots. My outer shirt, with a towel I made, by soaking off the paper of a picture that had a cloth back, and a blanket that I had kept I sent to my Captain and Lieutenant; I knew the man that I sent by, and thought I could trust. He came back from the marine Hospital where they were confined. I said, "did you see Captain Aigan?" "Yes, sir." "Did you give him the blanket and bundle?" "Yes, sir, I gave them into his own hands."

As we lay on the wharf waiting to embark, I sauntered a little to one side, where I saw a curious little steamer used for exploding torpedoes under ships. She was perhaps thirty feet long, cigar-shaped, and was entered from the top side. Extending in front were two long iron arms which were securely bolted to a pole, some ten or fifteen feet long, and on the end of the pole was an iron to which the torpedoes were fastened. The pole had been broken in some service, and she was being refitted.

We went on board the rebel steamer *Celt*,[2] at Chinn's wharf. A heavy battery had been erected here. About eight o'clock in the morning of Sept. 23, we were finally off. The day was fine. Placing myself so as to obtain a good view of the harbor and Sumter, I promised myself a great treat going to the truce ground. In a few moments we were all ordered into a small close room in the centre of the boat lighted from above. The door opened into a gangway running fore and aft. I at once saw the game and pretended not to hear the order, but a soldier came and helped me in such a manner that I had no excuse for holding back. I was the last to go in and stood in the door. The soldier pushed me back with his musket. I told him it was hot, and I wanted some air. He saw that I was looking at the city that lay behind us, and Castle Pinkney a little to the north[3]; he was a short man, and I looked over his head. The poor fellow straightened himself up and tried to interrupt my view, but his greatness in this world was not high enough for that. His superior officer standing by saw the state of the case, and sent another man to take his place. Having seen all that was to be seen in the direction of Charleston, I wished to see Fort Sumter. I heard the officer of the guard command the sentinel not to allow the "yanks" to look out at all. A new system of tactics must be adopted. The engine and machinery of the boat was in the open gangway, and I at once began to ask him questions about steam engines and the wonders of steam. Seeing that I was a poor benighted, ignorant "mudsill," his compassionate nature was moved, and he at once began to enlighten me on the subject. Such was the disposition of the torpedoes that ships going out must sail directly to Fort Sumter and then turn to the left and go north, etc. The officer had himself gone to get a view of Sumter, and while the soldier thought I listened to every word and was looking at the engine, I had a fine view of the famous fort lying before us and toward which we were sailing. The side toward the city was standing, but had been well perforated by Gen. Foster's shells and bolts. After passing we were allowed to come out, and the side of Sumter toward the sea was a heap of ruins. The north side of the harbor from Moultrie toward the city for miles was a continuous line of earthworks. Fort Moultrie was covered with sandbanks and new bastions.

Several wrecks were along the shore where the blockade runners came to sorrow. It was a gala day, and the works of both armies were covered with troops. Flags were floating in every direction. The inside fleet lay within the bar, and beyond the outer fleet lay, on the distant sea, monitors and ships of every class. It was a noble fleet, and a sight worth the seeing. Our boats came first on the truce ground, and came to anchor. Was there a mistake? Our hearts beat quick lest some unseen event should cause us to be sent back. Presently a large, elegant steamer from the southeast shot rapidly through the fleet, and sweeping a graceful circle came along side, and we were soon locked together. 'Twas the United States transport steamer *Delaware.* A large, elegant ship, clean, and everything in perfect trim. The *Celt* was a mean, little patched up, half painted one horse affair, and I felt almost ashamed to be exchanged from the deck of such a scrawny ship. The neatly dressed soldiers on the *Delaware* looked sweet enough to kiss. The guard over us—well, never mind. The mean, dirty rag of the rebellion floated from the mast of the *Celt,* while fifty feet above it from the lofty staff of the *Delaware* floated the stars and stripes, the glorious flag of the Union. It looked sweet as the face of an angel, and the hot tears of joy would come as I looked upon it. After the usual preliminaries we were transferred to the *Delaware.* Will I ever forget with what emotions I put my foot on that narrow gang plank? Col. Woodford, that Christian gentleman, stood at the end of the plank and took us each by the hand and gave us a cordial and hearty welcome.[4] God bless that good man. What a change! For almost five months no brotherly hand, save fellow prisoners, had been extended. His kindly words of love and welcome, his genial grasp, as in behalf of the government he said, "We are glad to receive you back, we congratulate you on behalf of your friends that you are alive and well." I shall not forget him. Presently the business of the truce was concluded, the boxes, bales and barrels in vast quantities put on board the *Celt* for the prisoners, and we parted; she to go back to her den, and we to move off to get into God's land among his people. When fairly off there was great joy among us.

We reached Hilton Head soon after dark, and in a few days left for New York and home. So far as I know, out of the fifty men who were captured with me, about forty-one have died. Captain Aigan and Lieutenant Durfee are out and safe. I joined my regiment again and remained till the expiration of the time for which I entered the service, and was then mustered out. On my return to Newbern I went back to the battle-field.[5] The bones of my horse lay where he fell. The hole in the skull showed where the ball went in that took his life. When the flag of truce went out I had on my person a fine pistol presented me, and I would not surrender it. I took up a sod in the fort and took out some earth and placed the pistol in the trench and covered it up. When I returned to the place I found it safe, save the marks of rust, and have it with me, and cherish it as an old friend. A few days since I met Captain Aigan, and asked him if he received the blanket and shirt I sent him as I left Charleston. He said no. The scamp I sent it by stole it!

The wear and suspense of my prison life wore more upon my home than me, and almost broke it up. While I walked by the dead line looking at the face of the heavens, thinking that their reflection would shine upon the roof above my loved ones. I found on reaching home that the small hours of morning often found my companion gazing at the cold moon and the stars, wondering whether they shone upon a cold grave or on one that should return. I am grateful to my God.

Patient reader, farewell. These papers are closed. I will tax your patience no more. I hope it has been less painful to you than to me were the weary months, some sketches of which I have laid before you."

*Zion's Herald and Wesleyan Journal,* June 14, 1865, p. 93.

# Epilogue

In 1865, after the war, White became an agent of the Freedman's Association of the Methodist Episcopal Church. The next year he transferred to the Detroit Conference of the Methodist Episcopal Church which appointed him to Ann Arbor, Michigan. After two successful years there, he transferred to the Wisconsin Conference, which appointed him to a Milwaukee church. During 1869–73, he was the Presiding Elder of the Fond Du Lac District.

Several months before the Annual Conference in 1873, considerable excitement erupted over reported deals in silver-mining stock in the far West. Several ministers, including White, were involved in these deals. At the conference, White, together with another minister, was charged in open conference with engaging in the stock transactions. They were both found guilty and suspended for one year from the ministry. An appeal was noted. The following year White located (i.e., removed himself from appointment) and apparently sent a long letter criticizing the actions of the 1873 conference (the letter is not extant). The conference accepted the location status but expressed disapproval of what it considered the unjustness of White's insinuations.

From 1878 to 1883, White was again reappointed to different churches in the Detroit Conference. In 1883 he retired; he died in 1916. The conference journal for that year, in its memorial obituary, said of White that "perhaps in all lives there is an especially prominent line of continuity of character. . . . In Brother White this line of continuity was determination. Two other supporting qualities were very evident, viz., faith and courage."[1] Certainly White's letters to the *Herald* reflected these qualities.

# Notes

## Notes to Introduction

1. See Bell I. Wiley, *The Life of Billy Yank* (Indianapolis: Bobbs-Merrill, 1952), 263–68; Bell I. Wiley, *The Life of Johnny Reb* (Indianapolis: Bobbs-Merrill, 1943), 186–91; Charles F. Pitts, *Chaplains In Gray* (Nashville: Broadman Press, 1957), 3–4, 7–9, 72–75; Sidney J. Romero, *Religion in the Ranks* (New York: University Press of America, 1983), 12–15.

2. Frederic Denison, *A Chaplain's Experience in the Union Army* (Providence: J. A. & R. A. Reid, 1879).

3. *Minutes of the Providence Conference of the Methodist Episcopal Church, 1855–1863; General Minutes of the Annual Conference, 1855–1863.* John K. Burlingame, comp., *History of the Fifth Rhode Island Heavy Artillery* (Providence: Snow & Farnham, 1892), 121, 124. The Methodist Biblical Institute moved to Boston and became the Boston Theological School in 1867, and was incorporated into Boston University in 1871.

4. Burlingame, *History of the Fifth*, 176.

5. J. Madison Drake, *Fast and Loose in Dixie* (New York: Author's Publishing Co., 1880), 41–54; Lieutenant A. Cooper, *In and Out of Rebel Prisons* (Oswego, N.Y.: R. J. Oliphant, 1888), 43–104; Willard W. Glazier, *The Capture and Prison Pen and the Escape* (Hartford: J. Munsell, 1868), 110–30; Captain J. J. Geer, *Behind the Lines* (Philadelphia: J. W. Daughaday, 1864), 93–106; J. V. Hadley, *Seven Months a Prisoner* (New York: Charles Scribner's Sons, 1898), 58–78; Lieutenant A. C. Roach, *The Prisoner of War and How Treated* (Indianapolis: Railroad City Publishing House, 1865), 123–25.

6. John McElroy, *This Was Andersonville* (New York: McDowell, Obolensky, 1957), 16. In May 1864, Major Thomas P. Turner wrote of 170 officers who had been at Andersonville for some months: "I do not believe any report has ever been made of them." *The War of the Rebellion: A Compilation of the Official Records of the Union and Confederate Armies,* 128 vols. (Washington, D.C.: GPO, 1880–1901), ser. 2, vol. 7: 167 (hereafter cited as *OR*).

7. *OR*, ser. 2, vol. 7: 472, 60–61, 585–86, 372–73.

8. The letters were first published, some in part and some in whole, in *The Georgia Historical Quarterly* 70 (Winter 1986): 669–702, and *Civil War History* 34 (March 1988): 22–45, and are reprinted herewith by kind permission of both journals.

## Notes to Letter 1

1. Burlingame, *History of the Fifth,* 208–17. White variously spells the town of Newbern and New Bern. The spelling in *OR* is New Berne.

2. In a September 1864 speech at Macon, Georgia, President Davis asserted that the men absent from the army without leave constituted one-third of the Confederate forces and that if just half of them returned to duty, the South could win the Civil War. Ella Lonn, *Desertion During the Civil War* (New York: Century Co., 1928), 31.

3. The Confederacy missed a golden opportunity by not using blacks as soldiers. After all, the South had a black population of 3,500,000, from which thousands of males could have been drawn. However, Georgia statesman Howell Cobb explained the deep reluctance of Confederate officials when he commented: "The day you make soldiers of them is the beginning of the end of the revolution. If slaves will make good soldiers, our whole theory of slavery is wrong." *OR,* ser. 4, vol. 3: 1009–10.

4. White's statement about blacks understanding the fundamental issues of the war was true. See Bell I. Wiley, *Southern Negroes, 1861-1865* (New Haven, Conn.: Yale University Press, 1938), 15–23.

5. According to John Ransom, however, if the election had occurred while he was in prison at Andersonville, four-fifths of the men would have voted for McClellan. They felt shamefully treated in being left so long as prisoners. John Ransom, *John Ransom's Andersonville Diary* (Middlebury, Vt.: John S. Eriksson, 1986), 166.

6. White's observations were correct, of course. State sovereignty was the cancer in the body politic. See James G. Randall, *Civil War and Reconstruction* (Boston: D. C. Heath and Co., 1937), 352–56.

7. Denison wrote that many prisoners from Andersonville were also released with White (*A Chaplain's Experience,* 39). Denison took White into his quarters and took care of his needs.

8. On April 20, 1864, Chaplain Dixon had been captured at Plymouth, North Carolina. He was paroled November 30, 1864, after which Dixon returned to his regiment for the last months of the war. Connecticut Adjutants-General, comp., *Record of Service of Connecticut Men in the Army and Navy of the United States During the War of the Rebellion* (Hartford, Conn.: Case, Lockwood & Brainard, 1889), 619.

## Notes to Letter 2

1. For more work on this forerunner of the YMCA, see Edward P. Smith, *Incidents of the United States Christian Commission* (Philadelphia: J. P. Lippincott & Co., 1869).

2. On February 19, 1865, Captain John Aigan escaped from prison. He returned to the 5th Rhode Island Heavy Artillery and on July 5, 1865, received promotion to major. Burlingame, *History of the Fifth,* 267.

3. Following his March 15, 1865, exchange, Lieutenant William H. Durfee, Jr., was mustered out of service. *Ibid.*

4. Sergeant Michael Kennedy died October 18, 1864, in a Charleston prison. *Ibid.,* 269.

5. Colonel Henry Sisson reported that "Captain White's horse was found dead in the ditch around the fort where he was shot." *OR,* vol. 36, pt. 2:5–6.

## Notes to Letter 3

1. "Col. Simon" is, of course, Colonel Henry T. Sisson, commander of the 5th Rhode Island Heavy Artillery. Colonel George N. Falk of the 6th North Carolina Cavalry was himself captured June 22, 1864, near Kinston. Falk spent the remainder of that year in Federal prisons.

2. Union casualties in the May 5 fight were three officers and forty-nine men captured, *OR,* vol. 36, pt. 2:6.

3. Falk's adjutant in the 6th North Carolina Cavalry was Lieutenant James H. Merrimon.

## Notes to Letter 4

1. White's observation was astute. "Confederate authorities knew that this service was the preferred branch and that the recruit would go to any length to provide himself a horse." E. Merton Coulter, *The Confederate States of America 1861–1865* (Baton Rouge: Louisiana State University Press, 1950), 339.

2. Captain Martin remains unidentified.

## Notes to Letter 5

1. Lieutenant Williamson remains unidentified.

2. According to Mrs. Frank Rouse, local historian of Kinston, White probably did observe a Presbyterian church service, but no Presbyterian church structure existed at that time. Rev. Harold J. Dudley, "History of the First Presbyterian Church, Kinston, N.C." (mimeographed, 1957). The author is indebted to Mrs. Rouse for confirming or slightly modifying all of White's observations at Kinston (personal letter to the author, March 3, 1987).

3. This was the ironclad ram *Neuse.* Robert MacBride, *Civil War Ironclads* (Philadelphia: Chilton Books, 1962), 102, and "Richard Caswell Memorial and the Ram Neuse," pamphlet, Division of Archives and History, North Carolina Historic Sites.

4. Brigadier General I. N. Palmer wrote of the *Neuse* that "a vessel like the one described could she get into the harbor, would do incalculable damage." *OR* 33:56.

5. Hope Bain was the Universalist minister serving Goldsboro and the surrounding area in 1864. *Universalist Companion and Almanac, 1864* (Boston: Abel Thompkins, 1864), 44.

6. For more on the mass execution of twenty-two Confederate deserters at Kinston, see *OR* 33:868–70; ser. 2, 6:1095; ser. 2, 8:903–4; Richard B. Harwell, ed., *The Confederate Reader* (New York: Longmans, Green, 1957), 263–71; Clifford Tyndall, "Lenoir County During the Civil War," (M.A. thesis, East Carolina State University, 1984, and privately published by the author), 73-82. The execution took place in the town square of Kinston, according to Mrs. Rouse.

## Notes to Letter 6

1. Edward D. Dill served his regiment for the remainder of the war and surrendered with the troops at Appomattox.

88

## Notes to Letter 8

1. White's impression of Wirz is consistent with that of other Union prisoners who later wrote of their experiences. John Ransom described Wirz: "Has a sneering sort of cast of countenance. Makes a fellow feel as if he would like to go up and boot him...a thoroughly bad man, without an atom of humanity about him." Ransom, *Diary,* 56, 92.

2. White underestimated the size of the Andersonville enclosure. The prison yard comprised 26½ acres. Ovid Futch, *Andersonville Prison* (Gainesville: University of Florida Press, 1968), 2.

## Notes to Letter 9

1. Ransom indicates that during the month of April, one in sixteen died; during May, one in twenty-six (more prisoners had arrived); by November, the death rate was one in three. Ransom, *Diary,* 281. See also Ovid Futch, "Prison Life at Andersonville," in *Civil War Prisons,* ed. William B. Hesseltine (Kent, Ohio: Kent State University Press, 1972), 9–31.

2. Ransom called these Union men "villains [who] live at the expense of so many" (*Diary,* 93) and gave a detailed description of their trial and execution by their fellow soldiers (105–18). Private Sylvester Hiscox also gave a detailed description of the raiders in Burlingame, *History of the Fifth,* 222–24.

3. Lieutenant Colonel Alexander W. Persons of the 57th Georgia was commandant of the Andersonville post until his June 1864 transfer.

4. Dr. Johnson is unidentified.

5. Futch, *Andersonville Prison,* 22, stated that contents of boxes were carefully examined and then delivered to the addresses. See letter 13, note 2, however, regarding pilferage of mail at Macon. It seems hardly likely that Andersonville would have been unlike Macon or Libby in this regard.

## Notes to Letter 10

1. Ransom also wrote of this ball, *Diary,* 79.

## Notes to Letter 11

1. William B. Hesseltine, *Civil War Prisons,* 159–64, provides an excellent picture of Macon that draws from the various personal reminiscences cited in Introduction, note 5.

2. The Macon prison, sometimes called "Camp Oglethorpe," occupied the Bibb County fairgrounds, a short distance from town. The prison consisted of a three-acre open field surrounded by a twelve-foot high wooden fence. Few buildings were within the enclosure, although prisoners were permitted to construct whatever shelters they could from scrap lumber and other materials brought to the prison for that purpose. Hesseltine, *Civil War Prisons,* 159–60; Geer, *Behind the Lines,* 93–94.

3. Major Thomas P. Turner found at Macon the same "gross mismanagement" and "want of system" that he had found at Andersonville. The highest number of Union officers ever reported incarcerated at Macon during the prison's short existence was fourteen hundred. *OR,* ser. 2, 7:167–69, 372–73, 418–19.

4. The words "fresh fish" were distinctive and used to distinguish the new prisoners from the old ones ("salt fish") at Libby Prison. The cry was always raised when new prisoners arrived and everyone ran to see who they were and what news they had. Drake, *Fast and Loose,* 41, used expressions almost identical to White. Glazier, *The Capture,* 112, said that after the first six months of prison life, when the officer was a "fresh fish," he served four months as a "sucker," the next two months as a "dry cod," the balance of the time as a "dried herring," and after exchange as a "pickled sardine."

5. Cooper, *In and Out,* 43, also commended Dixon for his spiritual services.

6. James F. Mackey of the 103d Pennsylvania had been captured April 20, 1864, at Plymouth, N.C.

## Notes to Letter 12

1. Money was sometimes a problem, however. Captain Tabb wrote to General Winder in Richmond on May 23, 1864, that many prisoners needed clothing and that the quartermaster at Richmond had money that belonged to them. The money was subsequently sent. *OR,* ser. 2, 7:158–59.

2. J. McCurdy, assistant surgeon and prisoner at Macon, after his release wrote to Washington, D.C., stating that "the wretched condition of these helpless officers beggars description. Most of them have been confined to their beds for four to twelve months, their bowels moving from one to three times each hour; crowded apartments. . ." *OR,* ser. 2, 7:908. Hessletine, *Civil War Prisons,* 160, stated that the men confined at Macon escaped the unhealthy conditions that prevailed at Andersonville because their numbers were fewer.

3. While food was severely rationed, none of the accounts of Macon voice harsh criticism at this point. Complaints consisted of husks in the cornmeal and rancid and maggot-infested bacon. Hesseltine, *Civil War Prisons,* 160, indicated that finding proper containers for storage was always a problem.

4. All previous letters had been signed H. S. White, Chaplain 5th Reg't R.I. Heavy Artillery. This letter and all subsequent letters were signed H. S. White.

## Notes to Letter 13

1. Brigadier General Henry W. Wessels began his Civil War service as colonel of the 8th Kansas. In April 1864, he was commanding the Federal garrison at Plymouth, N.C., when superior Confederate forces surrounded it. Following a four-month imprisonment, Wessels returned to duty as an administrative officer in Washington and New York.

2. Drake, *Fast and Loose,* 45, substantiated White's observations about mail at Macon: ". . . seldom did our keepers deliver to us the letters and papers sent us regularly from home."

He wrote that he would never forgive the Confederates for that. Cooper, *In and Out*, 98–102, also related the problems regarding mail at Macon.

## Notes to Letter 14

1. Major Bates remains unidentified.

2. In the spring of 1863, Colonel Abel D. Streight had slashed into Georgia with 1,700 Federal cavalry in an attempt to sever the railroads leading to and from Atlanta. General Nathan Bedford Forrest's Confederate troopers captured Streight's entire command on May 3 near the Alabama border.

3. In August 1864, Captain W. Kemp Tabb was captured on a train en route to Richmond. Federal authorities moved speedily to impose on Tabb "some of those indignities" that he allegedly had heaped upon Federal prisoners. *OR*, ser. 2, 7:582. Cooper, *In and Out*, 58, referred to Tabb as a cowardly rascal; and Roach, *The Prisoner of War*, 128, called him "cruel" and "vindictive."

## Notes to Letter 15

1. *Christian Index*, June 10, 1864, p. 97. The lengthy editorial does not mention White by name, but it is obvious from the comments and wording that White is the chaplain referred to by the writer.

2. The security of the Macon prison was never fully ensured. Digging escape tunnels became a routine pastime for the confined officer, but all personal accounts of soldiers at Macon indicate that spies and traitors prevented ultimate success of the endeavors.

3. Lieutenant Otto Gerson of the 44th New York.

4. Cooper, *In and Out*, 63, likewise noted that Belger was promoted to sergeant and wrote that the shooting of Gerson "was a BRUTAL AND DELIBERATE MURDER." Glazier, *The Capture*, 121, and Roach, *The Prisoner of War*, 130, called it, "murder in cold blood." Belger remains unidentified.

5. All accounts of July Fourth reinforce White's contention that it was a great day. Cooper, *In and Out*, 92, wrote that no officer who witnessed the celebration would ever forget it.

## Notes to Letter 16

1. Lieutenant Willson remains unidentified.

2. When a raid on the town by General George Stoneman's Federal forces appeared imminent in late July, all Macon prisoners were removed to Charleston or Savannah. See Ida Young, Julius Gholson, and Clara Nell Hargrove, *History of Macon, Georgia* (Macon: Lyon, Marshall & Brooks, 1950), 258–59.

3. Savannah-born Henry C. Wayne, Governor Joseph Brown stated, was the first Georgian to respond to the "call of his State when the dissolution of the Union was seen to be inevitable." Alexander A. Lawrence, *A Present for Mr. Lincoln* (Macon: Ardivan Press, 1961), 6.

## Notes to Letter 17

1. W. L. M. Burger, assistant adjutant general, on September 5, 1864 ordered firing to be altered so "the quarters of our prisoners of war now confined in Charleston will not be exposed, and the shells will drop in the most populous portion of the city." *OR,* vol. 35, pt. 2:272.

2. The "Swamp Angel" was an 8-inch Parrott gun with deadly long-range accuracy. However, it burst on the thirty-sixth discharge of fire into Charleston.

3. Sam Jones, major general, commanding, on September 10, 1864 enquired of Major General John G. Foster at Morris Island if Confederate officers were being put under fire in retaliation. He threatened to take immediate action if this was true and not corrected. *OR,* vol. 25, pt. 2:279.

## Notes to Letter 18

1. Colonel G. C. Gibbs, commanding, C.S. Military Prison, Macon, Georgia, requested that "Federal Chaplains be sent home, as they give a great deal of trouble." *OR,* ser. 2, 7:571. Major General Sam Jones wrote to Major General J. D. Foster, commanding at Hilton Head, that he had three chaplains as prisoners of war he wanted to send home. *Ibid.,* 696.

2. The *Celt* was a blockade runner. In September 1864 it was loaded and ready to sail when the Confederate commander in Charleston ordered it impounded for the use of carrying troops. It was "in good condition and capable of carrying 1,500 men at a trip." *OR,* vol. 35, pt. 2:624.

3. Castle Pinckney was a Charleston defensive work on a low-lying island only three-quarters of a mile from the mainland.

4. Lieutenant Colonel Jasper L. Woodford of the 127th New York was then serving as Provost Marshal General of the U.S. Department of the South.

5. White returned in a violent storm at Hatteras Inlet, November 9, 1864. Soon after Thanksgiving he told several companies at New Berne details of his capture and imprisonment. Burlingame, *History of the Fifth,* 242, 244.

## Notes to the Epilogue

1. *Minutes of the Wisconsin Conference 1873, 1874; Minutes of the Detroit Conference 1916; General Minutes of the Annual Conferences 1866–1916.*

# Index

Note: In references to notes, the letter number is in parentheses after the note number.

Aigan, Capt. John, 7–13, 15, 17, 20, 23, 26, 31, 37, 43, 51, 72, 81, 83–84
Andersonville (Georgia), prison at, 37–48
Augusta (Georgia), 35–36

Bain, Rev. Hope, 25–26
Bates, Maj., 62
Beauregard, Gen. P. G. T., 17, 28, 31
Belger, Sgt., 69
Bombing of prisoners of war, 79–80, 92 n. 1 (17)
Branchville (South Carolina), 1, 35
Brice's Creek (North Carolina), 7
Burger, Gen. W. L. M., 92 n. 1 (17)
Butler, Gen. Benjamin, 18

Camp Oglethorpe, 89 n. 2 (11)
Castle Pinckney, 82, 92 n. 3 (18)
Celt (ship), 1, 3, 82–83
Charleston (South Carolina), 1, 35, 78–82
Christian Commission, 6
Christian Index (Baptist newspaper), 66–67
Cobb, Gen. Howell, xiii, 87 n. 3 (1)
Croatan (North Carolina), 1, 6

Danites, 42, 89 n. 2 (9)
Davis, Jefferson, 3, 35, 48, 81, 87 n. 2 (1)

Dead line, 38–40, 55
Delaware (ship), 1, 83
Denison, Rev. Frederic, xi, 4, 87 n. 7 (1)
Dill, Rev. Edward, 28–30
Dixon, Rev. Charles, 4, 51–52, 54, 62–66, 69–70, 74, 76–77
"Dried herring," 90 n. 4 (11)
"Dry cod," 90 n. 4 (11)
Durfee, Lt. William, 7, 9, 12, 15, 23, 26, 37, 43, 51, 72, 81, 83

Evans Mill (North Carolina), 14

Falk, Col. George N., 11–12
Florence (South Carolina), 35
Fort Moultrie, 82
Fort Sumter, 82
Foster, Gen. J. D., 80, 82
Fourth of July celebration, 69–70, 91 n. 5 (15)
"Fresh fish," 50, 60

Gerson, Lt. Otto, 68
Gibbs, Col. G. C., 92 n. 1 (18)
Goldsboro (North Carolina), 1, 31
"Gopher holes," 68
Gordon (Georgia), 72

Hamburgh (South Carolina), 35
Hilton Head (South Carolina), 4, 83

"Johnnies," 68
Johnson, Dr., 43
Jones, Gen. Sam, 92 n. 3 (17), 92 n. 2 (18)

Kennedy, Sgt. Michael, 7–8
Kingsville (South Carolina), 35
Kinston (North Carolina), 1, 20–31; execution of Union troops at, 26–27

Libby Prison (Richmond, Virginia), 43, 60
Lincoln, Abraham, 2–3

Mackey, Capt. James F., 52, 54
McClellan, Gen. George, 2
McCurdy, Dr. J., 90 n. 2 (12)
McElroy, John, xiii
Macon (Georgia), 1, 36, 50; prison at, xii, 50–72
Martin, Capt., 19–20
Merrimon, Lt. James H., 88 n. 3 (3)
Millen (Georgia), 36
Morris Island (South Carolina), 80

Neuse River, 24; grounding of ship on, 24–25
New Berne (North Carolina), 1, 6, 13, 19, 26, 83

Palmer, Brig. Gen. I. N., 88 n. 4 (5)
Persons, Lt. Col. Alexander W., 42
"Pickled sardine," 90 n. 4 (11)
Pollocksville (North Carolina), 18

Raiders. *See* Danites
Ransom, John, 87 n. 5 (1), 89 n. 2 (9)

"Salt fish," 90 n. 4 (11)
Savannah (Georgia), prison at, 73–78
Sherman, Gen. William T., 70, 73
Simon, Col. *See* Sisson, Col. Henry T.
Sisson, Col. Henry T., 11, 87 n. 5 (2), 88 n. 1 (3)
Stoneman, Gen. George, 72, 91 n. 2 (16)
Streight, Col. Abel D., 64–65
"Sucker," 90 n. 4 (11)
"Swamp Angel," 80, 92 n. 2 (17)

Tabb, Capt. W. Kemp, 64–66, 68
Turner, Maj. Thomas P., 86 n. 6 (1), 90 n. 3 (11)

Wayne, Lt. Col. Henry C., 74
Wessels, Brig. Gen. Henry W., 58
White, Rev. Henry S.: appointed chaplain, Fifth Rhode Island Heavy Artillery, xi; capture of, 6–13; conducts prison religious services, xii, 24, 52, 62–66; early life and training, xi; on forced march, 14–20; postwar ministry, 85; prisoner at Andersonville, 37–48; prisoner at Charleston, 78–82; prisoner at Kinston, 20–31; prisoner at Macon; 50–72; prisoner at Savannah, 73–78; on prison food, 40–41, 56–59, 63; on prisoners' mail, 43–44, 60–61; on prison sanitation, 39–42, 55, 59–60; release and return home, 1, 3, 81–84, 92 n. 5 (18); on South and war, 2–3; on Southern slavery, 2, 28–30, 71–72
Williamson, Lt., 23, 88 n. 1 (5)
Willson, Lt., 72, 91 n. 1 (16)
Wilmington (North Carolina), 1, 33–34
Winder, Gen. John, xiii
Wirz, Capt. Henry, 89 n. 1 (8). *See also* Wurtz, Capt. Henry
Woodford, Lt. Col. Jasper L., 83
Wurtz, Capt. Henry, 37, 40–42. *See also* Wirz, Capt. Henry